Information System & Security

Dr. Ramchandra G Pawar
Principal, SVPM's College of Commerce, Science and
Computer Education, Malegaon, Tal – Baramati, Dist Pune

Rajnish Mishra
Assistant Professor, Dr. D. Y. Patil School of MCA,
Via Lohegaon (Bk), Charholi (BK), Pune

Dedicated to

Our beloved Teachers

1. Introduction to Information System

1.1 History of Information Systems Security

1.2 Importance of Information Systems & its basics

1.3 New Technologies open door to threats

1.4 Introduction to cyber crimes and attacks

1.5 Information Security: Threats & Attacks

1.6 Classification of Threats and Assessing Damages

Definitions:

A) **Information –**

1. Knowledge derived from study, experience, or instruction.

2. A collection of facts or data: statistical information.

3. Computer Science Processed, stored, or transmitted data.

4. Knowledge acquired through experience or study.

B) **Security –**

1. The state of being free from danger or threat

2. Freedom from risk or danger; safety

3. The protection of data to ensure that only authorized personnel has access.

4. Something that protects or makes safe; defense

C) Audit –

1. An examination of records or financial accounts to check their accuracy.

2. An adjustment or correction of accounts.

3. An examined and verified account.

4. An inspection of the accounting procedures and records.

D) Information security-

Information security is all about protecting and preserving information. It's all about protecting and preserving the confidentiality, integrity, authenticity, availability, and reliability of information.

1.1 The History Information system Security:-

The history of information security begins with the history of computer security. The need for computer security—that is, the need to secure physical locations, hardware, and software from outside threats—get up during World War-II when the first mainframes, developed to assist computations for communication code breaking, were information security put to use. Multiple levels of security were implemented to protect these mainframes and secure data integrity. Access to sensitive military locations was controlled through the use of devices, keys, and the facial recognition of authorized personnel by security guards. The growing need to maintain national security ultimately led to more complex and more technologically sophisticated computer security protections.

During these early years, information security was a straightforward process composed primarily of physical security and simple document classification schemes. The primary threats to security were physical theft of equipment, surveillance against the products of the systems, and damage.

a) History & Evaluation

Era -1960

One of the first documented security problems that were not physical in nature occurred in the early 1960s, when a systems administrator was working on a MOTD (message of the day) file, and another administrator was editing the password file. A software malfunction mixed the two files, and the entire password file was printed on every output file. During the Cold War, many more mainframes were brought online to achieve more complex and sophisticated tasks. It became necessary to find a way to enable these mainframes to communicate with each by means of a less bulky process than mailing magnetic tapes between computer centers. In response to this need, the Department of Defense's Advanced Research Project Agency (ARPA) began inspecting the feasibility of a redundant, networked communications system to support the military's exchange of information. Larry Roberts, known as the founder of the Internet, developed the project from its inception. This project, called ARPANET, is the origin of today's Internet.

Era 1970's and 80's

During this decade, the ARPANET became general and more widely used, and the potential for its misuse raised. In December of 1973, Robert M. "Bob" Metcalfe, who is recognized with the development of the Ethernet, one of the most popular networking protocols, identified fundamental problems with ARPANET security. Individual remote users' sites did not have adequate controls and safeguards to protect data from unauthorized remote users. Other problems overflowed: the vulnerability of password structure and formats; lack of safety procedures for dial-up connections; nonexistent user identification and authorization to the system. Because of the range and frequency of computer security violations and the explosion in the numbers of hosts and users on the ARPANET, network security was referred to as network insecurity.

The Rand Report R-609 was the first widely recognized published document to identify the role of management and policy issues in computer security. It noted that the wide use of networking components in information systems in the military introduced security risks that could not be mitigated by the routine practices then used to secure these systems.

Era 1990's

Networks of computers became more public, as did the need to connect these networks to each other. This gave rise to the Internet, the first global network of networks. This networking resource was made available to the general public in the 1990s, having previously been the domain of government, academia, and dedicated industry specialists. The Internet brought connectivity to virtually all computers that could reach a phone line or an Internet-connected local area network (LAN). After the Internet was commercialized, the technology became general, reaching almost every corner of the globe with an expanding array of uses. Since its inception as a tool for sharing Defense Department information, the Internet has become an interconnection of millions of networks. At first, these connections were based on de facto standards, because industry standards for interconnection of networks did not exist at that time.

Present Era

Today, the Internet brings millions of unsecured computer networks into continuous communication with each other. The security of each computer's stored information is now dependent on the level of security of every other computer to which it is connected.

a) **Critical characteristics of information:-**

Availability – enables authorized users – persons or computer systems-to access information without interference or obstruction and receive it in the required format.

Accuracy – Accuracy of information refers to information which is free from mistakes or errors and has the value the end user expects (Eg inaccuracy of your bank account may result in mistakes such as bouncing of a check)

Authenticity – refers to quality or state of being genuine or original, rather than reproduction or fabrication. Information is authentic when the contents are original as it was created, palced or stored or transmitted. (The information you receive as e-mail may not be authentic when its contents are modified what is known as E-mail spoofing)

Confidentiality – Information has confidentiality when disclosure or exposure to unauthorized individuals or systems is prevented Confidential it\ ensures that only those with the rights and privileges to access information are able to do so. When unauthorized individuals or systems can view information. Confidentiality is breached.

Integrity —Information has integrity when it is whole. Complete and uncorrupted the integrity of information is threatened when it is exposed to corruption, damage, destruction, other disruption of its authentic state. (Many computer viruses or worm are designed with the explicit purpose of corrupting data. Information integrity is the -corner stone of information systems. Because information is of no value or use if users cannot verify its integrity. Redundancy bits and check bits can compensate for internal and external threats to integrity of information.

Utility -The utility of information is the quality or state of having value for some purpose or end.

(For example.theUScensus data reveals information about the voters like their gender, age, race, and. so on.

Possession – the possession of information is the quality or state of having ownership or control of some object or item. Breach of possession does not result in breach of confidentiality.

b) Objectives of Information Security:-

- The goal of the ISM process is to align IT security with business security and ensure that information security is effectively managed in all service and service management activities

- ISM needs to be considered within the overall corporate governance framework

- Corporate governance is the set of responsibilities and practices exercised by the board and executive management with the goal of providing strategic direction, ensuring the objectives are achieved, ascertaining the risks are being managed appropriately, and verifying that the enterprise's resources are used effectively

- The purpose of ISM is to provide a focus for all aspects of IT security and manage all IT security activities

- The objective of ISM is to protect the interests of those relying on information, and the systems and communications that deliver the information from harm resulting from failures of availability, confidentiality, and integrity (CIA)

- The security objective is met when:

  - Information is available when needed (**Availability**)

  - Information is exposed only to authorized users (**Confidentiality**)

  - Information is complete and modified only through approved procedures (**Integrity**)

  - Business exchanges and information exchanges can be trusted (**Authenticity and non-repudiation**)

- The primary guide to defining what must be protected and the level of protection has to come from the business

In general, **security** is "the quality or state of being secure—to be free from danger". In other words, protection against adversaries—from those who would do harm, intentionally or otherwise—is the objective. National security, for example, is a multilayered system that protects the sovereignty of a state, its assets, its resources, and its people. Achieving the appropriate level of security for an organization also depends on a multifaceted system. A successful organization should have the following multiple layers of security in place to protect its operations:

- **Physical security-** to protect physical items, objects, or areas from unauthorized access and misuse.

- **Personal security-** to protect the individual or group of individuals who are authorized to access the organization and its operations.

- **Operations security-** to protect the details of a particular operation or series of activities.

- **Communications security-** to protect communications media, technology, and content.

- **Network security-** to protect networking components, connections, and contents.

- **Information security-** to protect information assets.

Information, software, hardware and networks are protected in three layers:

Products = physical-level security

-Ensuring physical security around the data – may be as basic as placing door locks or as

Complicated as installing intrusion-detection systems and firewalls (security hardware and software)

People = personnel-level security

-hiring most qualified individuals, providing necessary training, enforcing strict access control, terminating individuals in a way that protects all parties involved

Procedures and policies = organizational-level security

- required where product and people security are not sufficient – includes establishment of strategies that prevent any form of illegitimate activity and potential misuse of information

c) **The Need for Security :**

- Business Needs First, Technology Needs Last

- Information security performs four important functions for an organization

- Protects the organization's ability to function

- Enables the safe operation of applications implemented on the organization's IT systems

- Protects the data the organization collects and uses

- Safeguards the technology assets in use at the organization

- Protecting the Ability to Function

- Management is responsible o Information security is a management issue a people issue

- Communities of interest must argue for information security in terms of impact and cost

- Enabling Safe Operation

- Organizations must create integrated, efficient, and capable applications

- Organization need environments that safeguard applications

- Management must not abdicate to the IT department its responsibility to make choices and enforce decisions

Protecting Data

- One of the most valuable assets is data

- Without data, an organization loses its record of transactions and/or its ability to deliver value to its customers

- An effective information security program is essential to the protection of the integrity and value of the organization's data

Safeguarding Technology Assets

- Organizations must have secure infrastructure services based on the size and scope of the enterprise

- Additional security services may have to be provided

- More robust solutions may be needed to replace security programs the organization has outgrown

Threats

- Management must be informed of the various kinds of threats facing the organization

- A threat is an object, person, or other entity that represents a constant danger to an asset

- By examining each threat category in turn, management effectively protects its information through policy, education and training, and technology controls securing the components.

The computer can be either or both the subject of an attack and/or the object of an attack When a computer is-

-The subject of an attack, it is used as an active tool to conduct the attack

-The object of an attack, it is the entity being attacked.

d) Information Security CIA Triangle:-

Information security (InfoSec), as defined by the standards published by the Committee on National Security Systems (CNSS), formerly the National Security Telecommunications and Information Systems Security Committee (NSTISSC),is the protection of information and its critical elements, including the systems and hardware that use, store, and transmit that information. Information security includes the broad areas of information security management, computer and data security, and network security. To protect information and its related systems, organizations must implement such tools as policy, awareness, training and education, and technology. The NSTISSC model of information security evolved from a concept developed by the computer security industry known as the C.I.A. triangle.

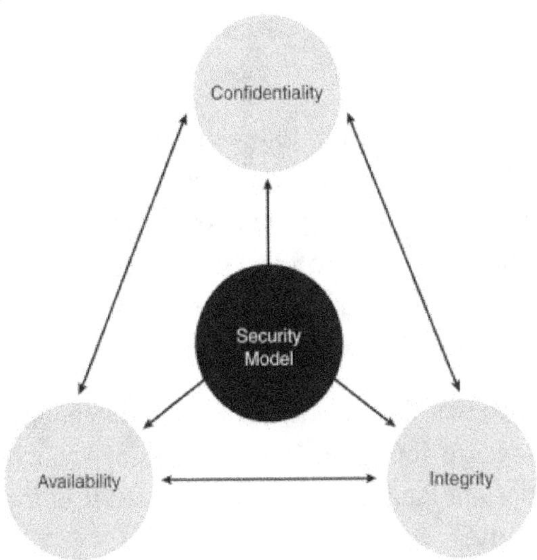

The **C.I.A.triangle**has been the industry standard for computer security since the development of the mainframe. It is based on the three characteristics of information that give it value for its use in organizations: confidentiality, integrity, and availability. The security of these three characteristics of information is as important today as it has always been, but the C.I.A. triangle model no longer adequately addresses the constantly changing environment of the computer industry. The threats to information confidentiality, integrity, and availability have evolved into a vast collection of events, including accidental or intentional damage, destruction, theft, unintended or unauthorized modification, or other misuses from human or nonhuman threats. This new environment of many constantly evolving threats has prompted the development of a more robust intellectual model.

The CIA principle

A simple but widely-applicable security model is the CIA triad; standing for Confidentiality, Integrity and Availability; three key principles which should be guaranteed in any kind of secure system. This principle is applicable across the whole subject of Security Analysis, from access to a user's internet history to security of encrypted data across the internet. If any one of the three can be breached it can have serious consequences for the parties concerned.

1. Confidentiality: Confidentiality is the ability to hide information from those people unauthorized to view it. It is perhaps the most obvious aspect of the CIA triad when it comes to security; but correspondingly, it is also the one which is attacked most often. Cryptography and Encryption methods are an example of an attempt to ensure confidentiality of data transferred from one computer to another.

2. Integrity:-The ability to ensure that data is an accurate and unchanged representation of the original secure information. One type of security attack is to intercept some important data and make changes to it before sending it on to the intended receiver.

3. Availability:-It is important to ensure that the information concerned is readily accessible to the authorized viewer at all times. Some types of security attack attempt to deny access to the appropriate user, either for the sake of inconveniencing them, or because there is some secondary effect. For example, by breaking the web site for a particular search engine, a rival may become more popular.

EXAMPLE-

- **Confidentiality:** Exam questions prior to exam must hidden from students.

- **Integrity:**Students grades must not be modified by students.

- **Availability:** Student schedules system must be online and available during the beginning of the semester.

Evaluation of Information Security:-

The objective of evaluation is to:

- Supervise and check compliance with the security policy and security requirements in SLAs and OLAs

- Carry out regular audits of the technical security of IT systems

- Provide information to external auditors and regulators, if required

1.2 Importance of Information Systems & its basics

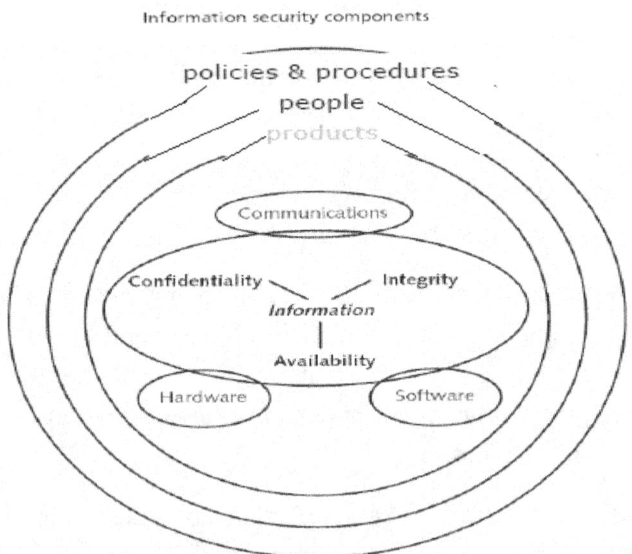

Components of Information System -

Components of an Information System

The 5 components that must come together in order to produce a Computer-Based Information system are:

1. Hardware: The term hardware refers to machinery. This category includes the computer itself, which is often referred to as the central processing unit (CPU), and all of its support equipments. Among the support equipment's are input and output devices, storage devices and communications devices.

2. Software: The term software refers to computer programs and the manuals that support them. Computer programs are machine-readable instructions that direct the circuitry within the hardware parts of the CBIS to function in ways that produce useful information from data. Programs are generally stored on some input / output medium, often a disk or tape.

3. Data: Data are facts that are used by programs to produce useful information. Like programs, data are generally stored in machine-readable form on disk or tape until the computer needs them.

4. Procedures: Procedures are the policies that govern the operation of a computer system. "Procedures are to people what software is to hardware" is a common analogy that is used to illustrate the role of procedures in a CBIS.

5. People: Every CBIS needs people if it is to be useful. Often the most over-looked element of the CBIS is the people, probably the component that most influence the success or failure of information systems.

1. Resources of people: (end users and IS specialists, system analyst, programmers, data administrators etc.).

2. Hardware: (Physical computer equipment's and associate device, machines and media).

3. Software: (programs and procedures).

4. Data: (data and knowledge bases), and

5. Networks: (communications media and network support).

People Resources

End users: (also called users or clients) are people who use an information system or the information it produces. They can be accountants, salespersons, engineers, clerks, customers, or managers. Most of us are information system end users.

• **IS Specialists:** people who actually develop and operate information systems. They include systems analysts, programmers, testers, computer operators, and other managerial, technical, and clerical IS personnel. Briefly, systems analysts design information systems based on the information requirements of end uses, programmers prepare computer programs based on the specifications of systems analysts, and computer operators operate large computer systems.

Hardware Resources

Machines: as computers and other equipment along with all data media, objects on which data is recorded and saved.Computer systems: consist of variety of interconnected peripheral devices. Examples are microcomputer systems, midrange computer systems, and large computer systems.

Software Resources

Software Resources includes all sets of information processing instructions. This generic concept of software includes not only the programs, which direct and control computers but also the sets of information processing (procedures).

Software Resources includes:

• System software, such as an operating system

• Application software, which are programs that direct processing for a particular use of computers by end users.

• Procedures, which are operating instructions for the people, who will use an information system. Examples are instructions for filling out a paper form or using a particular software package.

Data Resources

Data resources include data (which is raw material of information systems) and database. Data can take many forms, including traditional alphanumeric data, composed of numbers and alphabetical and other characters that describe business transactions and other events and entities. Text data, consisting of sentences and paragraphs used in written communications; image data, such as graphic shapes and figures; and audio data, the human voice and other sounds, are also important forms of data.

Network Resources

Telecommunications networks like the Internet, intranets, and extranets have become essential to the successful operations of all types of organizations and their computer-based information systems. Telecommunications networks consist of computers, communications processors, and other devices interconnected by communications media and controlled by communications software. The concept of Network Resources emphasizes that communications networks are a fundamental resource component of all information systems. Network resources include:

Communications media

Such as twisted pair wire, coaxial cable, fiber-optic cable, microwave systems, and communication satellite systems. • Network support: This generic category includes all of the people, hardware, software, and data resources that directly support the operation and use of a communications network. Examples include communications control software such as network operating systems and Internet packages.

1.3 New Technologies open door to threats

Challengaes:

- Protection of information and information systems to meet business and legal requirements.

- Provision and demonstration of secure environment to clients

- Preventing loss of product knowledge to external

- Preventing leak of confidential information

- Ease of access to large mobile work force

- Introduction of new technologies and tools

- Disaster recovery & Business continuity

- Managing legal compliance

- Managing costs v/s risk

- Information Security is the protection of information from a wide range of threats in order to ensure business continuity, minimize business risk, and maximize return on investments and business opportunities.

- Information security is achieved by implementing a suitable set of controls, policies, processes, procedures, organizational structures and software and hardware functions – to ensure that the specific security and business objectives are met.

- Organizations and their information systems and networks are faced with security threats from a wide range of sources, including.

ISMS

- ISMS provides a framework to establish, implement, operate,monitor, review,maintain and improve the information security within an organization

- ISMS provides means to

- ❏ Manage risks to suit the business activity

- ❏ Manage incident handling activities

- ❏ Build a security culture

- ❏ Conform to the requirements of the Standard

Who need ISMS

- Every organisation which values information needs to protect it e.g.

- Banks

- Call centers

- IT companies

- Government ¶statal bodies

- Manufacturing concerns

- Hospitals

- Insurance companies

Who get Benefits?

- Assurance through discipline of compliance

- Risk management

- Secure environment (protection of IPRs)

- Minimize security breaches (continuity of business)

- Increase trust & customer confidence & business opportunities

Why it Need?

- ❏ Computer-assisted fraud

- ❏ Sabotage

- ❏ Vandalism

- ❑ Fire or flood

- ❑ Hacking

- ❑ Denial of service attacks

Objectives

- ❑ Preservation of information

- ❑ Confidentiality: ensuring that information is available to only those authorised to have access

- ❑ Integrity: Safeguarding the accuracy and completeness of information & processing methods

- ❑ Availability: ensuring that information and vital services are available to authorised users when required.

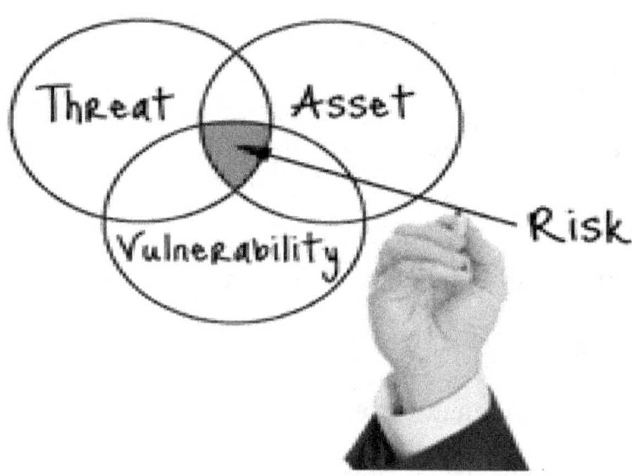

Risk Analysis has been defined as:"a formal process of determining risks and developing a plan to deal with them". Risks do not arise all by themselves. A risk is normally a product of two factors: threats (something could go wrong) and vulnerabilities (the information system/s used by the business will allow things to do wrong).

Threats include:-

- Deliberate manipulation of information prior to input/processing
- Impersonation of a legitimate user

- Untrained or poorly trained staff

Vulnerabilities include:-

- Poor website or network design

- Poor recruitment procedures

The first - and key stage - in addressing risks is to do a risk analysis:

A risk analysis process has three main stages:

(1) Understanding risks to the business and how they can occur
(2) Understanding the potential cost to the business if they do occur
(3) Identifying suitable and effective measures and policies to: -Minimize the likelihood of the threats happening   -Prevent or detect the threat   - Enable appropriate recovery action to be taken

Many risks can be quantified - since they occur in most businesses - and there is lots of evidence of how threats and vulnerabilities arise. The most important element in the process is that risk decisions are taken openly. Denying the presence of risk is not helpful. But trying to reduce the risk to zero is not realistic, and will normally cost more than it will save.

1.4 Introduction to cyber crimes and attacks

Cyber-crime is an evil having its origin in the growing dependence on computers inmodern life. In a day and age when everything from microwave ovens and refrigerators to nuclear power plants is being run on computers, cybercrime has assumed rather evil implications.

Definition of Cyber Crime- Computer crime can involve criminal activities that are traditional in nature, such as theft, fraud, forgery, defamation and mischief, all of which are subject to the Indian Penal Code. The abuse of computers has also given birth to a gamut of new age crimes that are addressed by the Information Technology Act, 2000.

Defining cyber-crimes, as "acts that are punishable by the Information Technology Act" would be unsuitable as the Indian Penal Code also covers many cyber-crimes, such as email spoofing and cyber defamation, sending threatening emails etc. A simple yet sturdy definition of cyber-crime would be "unlawful acts wherein the computer is either a tool or a target or both".

Major cyber-crimes in the past include the Citibank rip off. US $ 10 million were fraudulently transferred out of the bank and into a bank account in Switzerland. A Russian hacker group led by Vladimir Kevin, a renowned hacker, perpetrated the attack. The group compromised the bank's security systems. Vladimir was allegedly using his office computer at AO Saturn, a computer firm in St. Petersburg, Russia, to break into Citibank computers. He was finally arrested on Heathrow airport on his way to Switzerland.

The first recorded cyber-crime took place in the year 1820! That is not surprisingconsidering the fact that the abacus, which is thought to be the earliest form of acomputer, has been around since 3500 B.C. in India, Japan and China. The era ofmodern computers, however, began with the analytical engine of Charles Babbage.

The kind of activity usually involves a modification of a conventional crime by using Computers.

Some examples are:

Financial crimes:-

This would include cheating, credit card frauds, money laundering etc. To cite are cent case, a website offered to sell Alphonso mangoes at a throwaway price. Distrusting such a transaction, very few people responded to or supplied the website with their credit card numbers. These people were actually sent the Alphonso mangoes. The word about this website now spread like wildfire. Thousands of people from all over the country responded and ordered mangoes by providing their credit card numbers. The owners of what was later proven to be a bogus website then fled taking the numerous credit card numbers and proceeded to spend huge amounts of money much to the chagrin of the card owners.

Cyber pornography:-

This would include pornographic websites; pornographic magazines produced using computers (to publish and print the material) and the Internet (to download and transmit pornographic pictures, photos, writings etc.).

One incident, in Mumbai a Swiss couple would gather slum children and then would force them to appear for obscene photographs. They would then upload these photographs to websites specially designed for paedophiles. The Mumbai police arrested the couple for pornography.

Sale of illegal articles:–

This would include sale of narcotics, weapons and wildlife etc., by posting informationon websites, auction websites, and bulletin boards or 167 simply by using emailommunication. E.g. many of the auction sites even in India are believed to beselling cocaine in the name of 'honey'.

Online gambling:–

There are millions of websites; all hosted on servers abroad, that offer online gambling. In fact, it is believed that many of these websites are actually fronts for money laundering.

Intellectual Property crimes:-

These include software piracy, copyright infringement, trademarks violations, theft of computer source code etc.

Email spoofing:-

A spoofed email is one that appears to originate from one source but actually has been sent from another source. E.g. Pooja has an e-mail addresspooja@asianlaws.org. Her enemy, Sameer spoofs her e-mail and sends obscene messages to all her acquaintances. Since the e-mails appear to have originated from Pooja, her friends could take offence and relationships could be spoiled for life. Email spoofing can also cause monetary damage.

Forgery:-

Counterfeit currency notes, postage and revenue stamps, mark sheets etc. can beforged using sophisticated computers, printers and scanners. Outside many colleges across India, one finds touts soliciting the sale of fake mark sheets or even certificates. These are made using computers, and high quality scanners and printers. In fact, this has becoming a booming business involving thousands of Rupees being given to student gangs in exchange for these bogus but authentic looking certificates.

Cyber Defamation:–

This occurs when defamation takes place with the help of computers and / or the Internet. E.g. someone publishes defamatory matter about someone on a website or sends e-mails containing defamatory information to all of that person's friends.

In reality, a group of people displeased with her views and angry with her for opposing they had decided to get back at her by using such underhanded methods. In addition to sending spoofed obscene e-mails they also put up websites about her, that basically malignedher character and sent e-mails to her family and friends containing matter defaming her.

Cyber stalking:–

The Oxford dictionary defines stalking as "pursuing stealthily". Cyber stalking involves following a person's movements across the Internet by posting messages (sometimes threatening) on the bulletin boards frequented by the victim, entering the chat-rooms frequented by the victim, constantly bombarding the victim with emails etc.

Unauthorized access to computer systems or networks:–

This activity is commonly referred to as hacking. The Indian law has however given a different connotation to the term hacking, so we will not use the term "unauthorized access" interchangeably with the term "hacking".

Theft of information contained in electronic form:-

This includes information stored in computer hard disks, removable storage media etc.

Email bombing:-

Email bombing refers to sending a large number of emails to the victim resulting inthe victim's email account (in case of an individual) or mail servers (in case of a company or an email service provider) crashing. In one case, a foreigner who had been residing in Simla, India for almost thirty years wanted to avail of a scheme introduced by the Simla Housing Board to buy land at lower rates. When he made an application it was rejected on the grounds that the 169 schemes was available only for citizens of India. He decided to take his revenge. Consequently he sent thousands of mails to the Simla Housing Board and repeatedly kept sending e-mails till their servers crashed.

Data diddling:-

This kind of an attack involves altering raw data just before it is processed by a computer and then changing it back after the processing is completed. Electricity Boards in India have been victims to data diddling programs inserted when private parties were computerizing their systems.

Salami attacks:–

These attacks are used for the commission of financial crimes. The key here is to make the alteration so insignificant that in a single case it would go completely unnoticed. E.g. a bank employee inserts a program, into the bank's servers, that deducts a small amount of money (say Rs. 5 a month) from the account of every customer. No account holder will probably notice this unauthorized debit, but the bank employee will make a sizable amount of money every month.

It was brought to their notice when a person by the name of Zygler opened his account in that bank. He was surprised to find a sizable amount of money being transferred into his account every Saturday.

Denial of Service attack:-

This involves flooding a computer resource with more requests than it can handle. This causes the resource (e.g. a web server) to crash thereby denying authorized users the service offered by the resource. Another variation to a typical denial of service attack is known as a Distributed Denial of Service (DDoS) attack wherein the perpetrators are many and are geographically widespread. It is very difficult to control such attacks. The attack is initiated by sending excessive demands to the victim's computer(s), exceeding the limit that the victim's servers can support and making the server's crash. Denial-of-service attacks have had an impressive history having, in the past, brought down websites like Amazon, CNN, Yahoo and eBay.

Virus / worm attacks:-

Viruses are programs that attach themselves to a computer or a file and then circulate themselves to other files and to other computers on a network. They usually affect the data on a computer, either by altering or deleting it. Worms, unlike viruses do not need the host to attach themselves to. They merely make functional copies of themselves and do this repeatedly till they eat up all the available space on a computer's memory.

Logic bombs:-

These are event dependent programs. This implies that these programs are created to do something only when a certain event (known as a trigger event) occurs. E.g. even some viruses may be termed logic bombs because they lie dormant all through the year and become active only on a particular date (like the Chernobyl virus).

Trojan attacks:-

A Trojan as this program is aptly called is an unauthorized program which functions from inside what seems to be an authorized program, thereby concealing what it is actually doing. There are many simple ways of installing a Trojan in someone's computer. To citeand example, two friends Rahul and Mukesh (names changed), had a heated argument over one girl, Radha (name changed) whom they both liked. When the girl, asked to choose, chose Mukesh over Rahul, Rahul decided to get even. On the14th of February, he sent Mukesh a spoofed e-card, which appeared to have come from Radha's mail account. The e-card actually contained a Trojan. As soon as Mukesh opened the card, the Trojan was installed on his computer. Rahul now had complete control over Mukesh's computer and proceeded to harass him thoroughly.

Internet time thefts:-

This connotes the usage by an unauthorized person of the Internet hours paid for by another person. In a case reported before the enactment of the Information Technology Act, 2000 Colonel Bajwa, a resident of New Delhi, asked a nearby net café owner to come and set up his Internet connection. For this purpose, the net café owner needed to know his username and password. After having set up the connection he went away with knowing the present username and password. He then sold this information to another net café. One week later Colonel Bajwa found that his Internet hours were almost over. Out of the 100 hours that he had bought, 94 hours had been used up within the span of that week. Surprised, he reported the incident to the Delhi police. The police could not believe that time could be stolen.

Web jacking:-

This occurs when someone forcefully takes control of a website.. The actual owner of the website does not have any more control over what appears on that website. In a recent incident reported in the USA the owner of a hobby website for children received an e-mail informing her that a group of hackers had gained control over her website. They demanded a ransom of1 million dollars from her. The owner, a schoolteacher, did not take the threat seriously. She felt that it was just a scare tactic and ignored the e-mail. It was three days later that she came to know, following many telephone calls from all over the country, that the hackers had web jacked her website. Subsequently, they had altered a portion of the website which was entitled 'How to have fun with goldfish'. In all the places where it had been mentioned, they had replaced the word 'goldfish' with the word 'piranhas'. Piranhas are tiny but extremely dangerous flesh-eating fish. Many children had visited the popular website and had believed what the contents of the website suggested. These unfortunate children followed the instructions, tried to play with piranhas, which they bought from pet shops, and were very seriously injured!

Theft of computer system:-

This type of offence involves the theft of a computer, some part(s) of a computer or a peripheral attached to the computer.

Physically damaging a computer system:-

This crime is committed by physically damaging a computer or its peripherals

1.5 Threats to Information Security

The threats to information security come from methods of attack developed in order to exploit IT vulnerabilities, or cause harm to a network or computer system. They come in many forms:

Complacency -

This is the biggest threat to any IT system. All IT systems and networks should be run by people who are not going to take the matter of security lightly. In order to abide by privacy laws, a computer system and network must have adequate protection.

Ignorance -

Nobody says you need to be an IT expert in order to protect your IT systems, but being completely ignorant of IT security is another big threat to the integrity of your system.

Over-zealous behavior -

At the other end of the spectrum are people who are so afraid of IT threats that they purchase and download anything they think will help their security? They purchase malware programs that are disguised as virus checkers and compromise their own security.

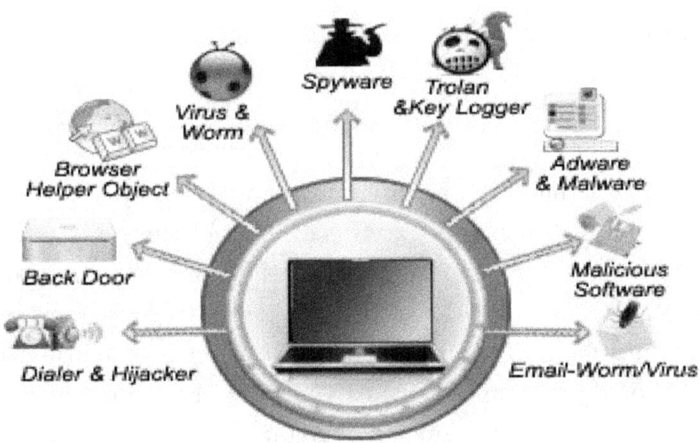

Exploit scripts–

Your FTP information is read by a program that sends it to another site. If you visit this site, you fall foul of a virus that attacks or steals from your system.

Worms, viruses, rootkits, Trojans–

These are created by people who wish to gain access to your IT system. Sometimes they want to steal the information held on your computer, but more often than not they want access to accounts that your system uses. Sometimes, someone will want access to your system in order to terrorize other systems. For example, a piece of malware could be installed into 1000 computers, which will make them visit a website repeatedly all at the same time. Doing this will crash the website, and the hacker/programmer will threaten such attacks if his or her demands are not met.

Downloads–

Downloading anything will pose a risk to your computer system, and in many cases, you need a virus checker in order to find out if the thing you download is safe or not.

Installations–

Installing new things such as programs and patches is very dangerous. Sometimes a program can fool a virus checker because it is safe — until it is unpacked and installed. This is why installations are very dangerous, especially since you often have to agree to allow a program to change your computer before it will install. Some form of patch management software should be installed. One of your best protections against this is a good system restore program and good quality security patches.

Counteracting Possible Threats–

Make sure that your system is updated as often as possible. Make sure you have a good patch management and patch deployment system.

You must lessen the threat of a security breach with security protocols and malware checkers. Set up security protocols for yourself and your staff. Set rules for everything from emailing to windows patch management.

You must make sure that you and your entire staff are up to date on current security issues and patch management policy. Lessen the damage of a security breach by making backup copies of your valuable information.

1.6 Classification of Threats and Assessing Damages

Threats to Information Security

Categories of threat	Examples
1. Acts of human error or failure	Accidents, employee mistakes
2. Compromises to intellectual property	Piracy, copyright infringement
3. Deliberate acts of espionage or trespass	Unauthorized access and/or data collection
4. Deliberate acts of information extortion	Blackmail of information disclosure
5. Deliberate acts of sabotage or vandalism	Destruction of systems or information
6. Deliberate acts of theft	Illegal confiscation of equipment or information
7. Deliberate software attacks	Viruses, worms, macros, denial-of-service
8. Forces of nature	Fire, flood, earthquake, lightning
9. Deviations in quality of service from service providers	Power and WAN service issues
10. Technical hardware failures or errors	Equipment failure
11. Technical software failures or errors	Bugs, code problems, unknown loopholes
12. Technological obsolescence	Antiquated or outdated technologies

Critical infrastructures in around the world have for some time been the target of cyber-related attacks for criminal, political or other motives. CSIS broadly defines a cyber-related attack as the use of information systems or computer technology either as a weapon or a target. Hostile actors could include individuals acting on their own, hacktivists, intelligence agencies and terrorists. Regardless of their motivations, hostile actors have potential access to a growing range (various tools and techniques) that could be used to engage in malicious activity directed against the computer-related components of the critical infrastructure.

Recent media reporting on cyber security issues continues to illustrate the impacts of cyber-related operations directed against public and private sector systems worldwide, noting the use of crafted e-mails, social networking services and other means and techniques to facilitate efforts of various hostile actors to acquire government, corporate or personal data. These tools and techniques are becoming more complex and difficult to detect.

2. Information Security Management in Organizations

2.1 Information Security in Organization

2.2 Security Policy,

2.3 Standards,

2.4 Guidelines & Procedures

2.5 ISMS

2.6 The 3 pillars CIA of Information Security

2.7 Information Classification

2.8 Risk Analysis & Management

2.1 Information Security in Organization:

The information is one of most valuable assets of the organization. Therefore, the relevant system namely Information Security Management System (ISMS) is very important part of business management system of every organization. The main objectives of ISMS are to ensure the confidentiality, integrity and availability of the information in the organization. The access to the information asset is managed through the special rules, according to the roles and privileges. The importance of the unified process of information security management determines the creation of standard mechanisms and procedures and special organizational structures for its implementation. The basic activities include also the means and tools for the deployment, monitoring, analysis, maintenance and modification of the ISMS. Moreover, the significance of the information security for business success in concurrency environment requires certification and accreditation of these systems.

Information is an asset, and having specific, relevant and correct information can make a massive difference to an organization's efficiency. With the huge number of available technologies; it is possible for information to be collected, shared, sold, exchanged and distributed without citation or notice to the owner. It is necessary to ensure information security so that it becomes a natural phase in the daily activities of an organization. Organizations must define the threats and vulnerabilities to their information resources to ensure the confidentiality, integrity and availability there of.

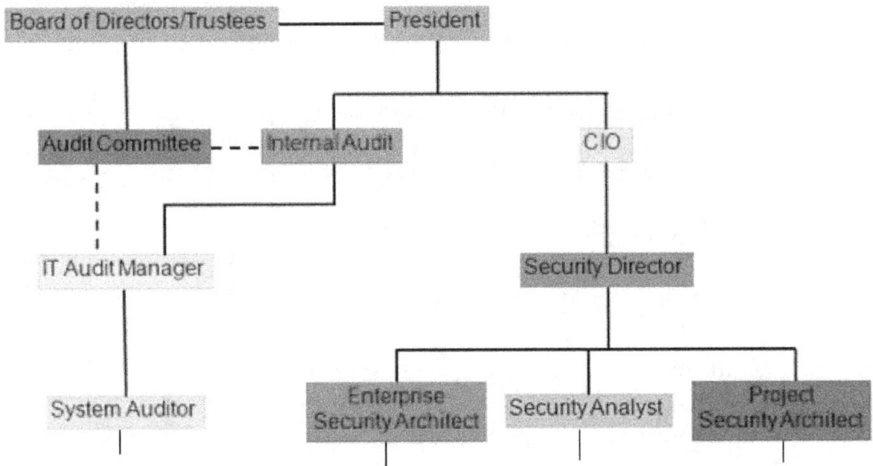

- Organizations have an internal value chain and must interact with external entities at either end of this chain.

- External entities may be other businesses, individual customers, or the government.

- Interactions must be protected from being compromised by unauthorized parties. Privacy deals with the degree of control that an entity, whether a person or organization, has over information about itself.

- Security deals with vulnerability to unauthorized access to content.

- It is difficult to connect security security-related expenditures to profitability

- Increases in security will often increase costs and reduce efficiency

- Security is not a technical issue; it is a management issue

- Total security is a myth.

- Not all information is of equal value

- it is not technically possible to protect all information assets

- Value of the firm's intellectual property

- The degree of change the firm is facing

- Its accessibility

- Its industry position

- Culture

- Education, Training, and Awareness.

2.2 Information Security Policy:

Information security policies provide vital support to security professionals as they strive to reduce the risk profile of a business and fend off both internal and external threats.

The trouble is that very few organizations take the time and trouble to create decent policies; instead they are happy to download examples from the web and cut and paste as they see fit. The resultant mess is no good to anyone, and can often leave the business open to unforeseen issues.

Information security policy is a set of policies issued by an organization to ensure that all information technology users within the domain of the organization or its networks comply with rules and guidelines related to the security of the information stored digitally at any point in the network or within the organization's boundaries of authority.

Every organization needs to protect its data and also control how it should be distributed both within and without the organizational boundaries. This may mean that information may have to be encrypted, authorized through a third party or institution and may have restrictions placed on its distribution with reference to a classification system laid out in the information security policy.

A typical security policy might be hierarchical and apply differently depending on whom they apply to. For example, the secretarial staff who type all the communications of an organization are usually bound never to share any information unless explicitly authorized, whereby a more senior manager may be deemed authoritative enough to decide what information produced by the secretaries can be shared, and to who, so they are not bound by the same information security policy terms. To cover the whole organization therefore, information security policies frequently contain different specifications depending upon the authoritative status of the persons they app.

The typical information security policy may have the following headings:

- Document Control

- Document Location

- Revision History

- Approvals

- Distribution

- Document History

- Enquiries

- Introduction and Purpose

- Scope

- Your Responsibilities

- Our Responsibilities

- Where to find more information

- Equal Opportunities Impact Assessment

This provides a more structured and accessible document.

Policy Definition-

A security policy is a document that outlines the rules, laws and practices for computer network access. This document regulates how an organization will manage, protect and distribute its sensitive information (both corporate and client information) and lays the framework for the computer-network-oriented security of the organization.

In business, a security policy is a document that states in writing how a company plans to protect the company's physical and information technology (IT) assets. A security policy is often considered to be a "living document", meaning that the document is never finished, but is continuously updated as technology and employee requirements change. A company's security policy may include an acceptable use policy, a description of how the company plans to educate its employees about protecting the company's assets, an explanation of how security measurements will be carried out and enforced, and a procedure for evaluating the effectiveness of the security policy to ensure that necessary corrections will be made.

I. **Policy**

A. It is the policy of ORGANIZATION XYZ that information, as defined hereinafter, in all its forms--written, spoken, recorded electronically or printed--will be protected from accidental or intentional unauthorized modification, destruction or disclosure throughout its life cycle. This protection includes an appropriate level of security over the equipment and software used to process, store, and transmit that information.

II. Scope

A. The scope of information security includes the protection of the confidentiality, integrity and availability of information.

B. The framework for managing information security in this policy applies to all ORGANIZATION XYZ entities and workers, and other Involved Persons and all Involved Systems throughout ORGANIZATION XYZ as defined below in INFORMATION SECURITY DEFINITIONS.

C. This policy and all standards apply to all protected health information and other classes of protected information in any form as defined below in INFORMATION CLASSIFICATION.

III. Risk Management

A. A thorough analysis of all ORGANIZATION XYZ information networks and systems will be conducted on a periodic basis to document the threats and vulnerabilities to stored and transmitted information. The analysis will examine the types of threats – internal or external, natural or manmade, electronic and non-electronic-- that affect the ability to manage the information resource. The analysis will also document the existing vulnerabilities within each entity which potentially expose the information resource to the threats. Finally, the analysis will also include an evaluation of the information assets and the technology associated with its collection, storage, dissemination and protection.

From the combination of threats, vulnerabilities, and asset values, an estimate of the risks to the confidentiality, integrity and availability of the information will be determined. The frequency of the risk analysis will be determined at the entity level.

B.   Based on the periodic assessment, measures will be implemented that reduce the impact of the threats by reducing the amount and scope of the vulnerabilities

Security Lifecycle

Like any other IT process, security can follow a lifecycle model. The model presented here follows the basic steps of IDENTIFY – ASSESS – PROTECT –MONITOR. This lifecycle provides a good foundation for any security program. Using this lifecycle model provides you with a guide to ensure that security is continually being improved. A security program is not a static assessment or finished product. Rather it requires constant attention and continual improvement. As with any other aspect of a security program, implementing the security lifecycle requires that policy and standards be implemented first. Security policy and standards are the foundation to any component of a security plan. These are especially critical in both the assessment and protection phase of the lifecycle. The assessment phase will use the standards and policy as the basis of conducting the assessment. Resources will be evaluated against the security policy. During the protection phase, resources will be configured to meet policy and standards.

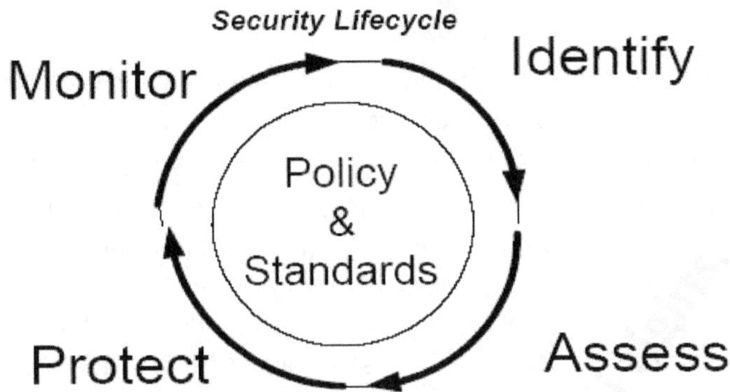

It demonstrates that the Security Lifecycle is built around security policy and standards. Now, let's take a look at each phase of the lifecycle and examine what is involved.

Identify–

The very first step in any security program is to know what it is that you are trying to protect. How can you protect an asset if you don't know anything about it? Or you don't even know that it exists. You need to map out your network, identify servers and understand what applications are running on them. The identification phase needs to start at the high level and drill down. You need to have a good understanding of the resources that you are trying to protect. Here are some questions to consider when trying identifying your enterprise resources.

- ✓ Where are the assets physically located? Are they in a secured datacenter or scattered about multiple office locations?
- ✓ How many servers, firewalls and routers do you have?
- ✓ What flavor of OS is running on each system?
- ✓ What applications and services are running on each server?
- ✓ Who is the customer for each system? Does the application support theHR, finance or the marketing department?
- ✓ What is the priority of the application? Is this a front end customer application or an internal, third tier application?

Assess:-

The assessment phase of the Security Lifecycle builds on the identification phase. Once the assets have been identified, the next step is to perform a thorough security assessment. The assessment phase can encompass many different aspects from reviewing processes and procedures to vulnerability scanning.

So if you have a large organization with hundreds of servers – where do you start? The answer is to prioritize! Evaluate the asset and consider the potential risk associated with each component. Start by carefully examining those servers that have the most risk and exposure -- those that are the most critical to your organization. It only makes sense to begin with those network components that have the most exposure – those facing the Internet or other external interfaces. When examining these servers, because they provide critical services for your enterprise, you.

2.5 ISMS:

An information security management system (ISMS) is a set of policies and procedures for systematically managing an organization's sensitive data. The goal of ISMS is to minimize risk and ensure business continuity by pro-actively limiting the impact of a security breach.

An ISMS typically addresses employee behavior and processes as well as data and technology. It can be targeted towards a particular type of data, such as customer data, or it can be implemented in a comprehensive way that becomes part of the company's culture.

ISO 27001 is a specification for creating ISMS. It does not mandate specific actions, but includes suggestions for documentation, internal audits, continual improvement, and corrective and preventive action.

Challenges:

❑ Protection of information and information systems to meet business and legal requirements.

❑ Provision and demonstration of secure environment to clients

❑ Preventing loss of product knowledge to external

❑ Preventing leak of confidential information

❑ Ease of access to large mobile work force

❑ Introduction of new technologies and tools

❑ Disaster recovery & Business continuity

❑ Managing legal compliance

❑ Managing costs v/s risk

❑ Information Security is the protection of information from a wide range of threats in order to ensure business continuity, minimize business risk, maximize return on investments and business opportunities.

❑ Information security is achieved by implementing a suitable set of controls, policies, processes, procedures, organizational structures and software and hardware functions – to ensure that the specific security and business objectives are met.

- Organizations and their information systems and networks are faced with security threats from a wide range of sources, including

ISMS

- ISMS provides a framework to establish, implement, operate, monitor, review, maintain and improve the information security within an organization

- ISMS provides means to

- Manage risks to suit the business activity

- Manage incident handling activities

- Build a security culture

- Conform to the requirements of the Standard

Who need ISMS

- Every organization which values information needs to protect it e.g.

- Banks

- Call centers

- IT companies

- Government ¶statal bodies

- Manufacturing concerns

- Hospitals

- Insurance companies

Who get Benefits?

- Assurance through discipline of compliance

- Risk management

- Secure environment (protection of IPRs)

- Minimize security breaches (continuity of business)

- Increase trust & customer confidence & business opportunities

Why it Needs ?

- Computer-assisted fraud

- Sabotage

- Vandalism

- Fire or flood

- Hacking

- Denial of service attacks

Objectives

- Preservation of information

- Confidentiality: ensuring that information is available to only those authorized to have access

- Integrity: Safeguarding the accuracy and completeness of information & processing methods

- Availability: ensuring that information and vital services are available to authorized users when required.

Components of ISMS

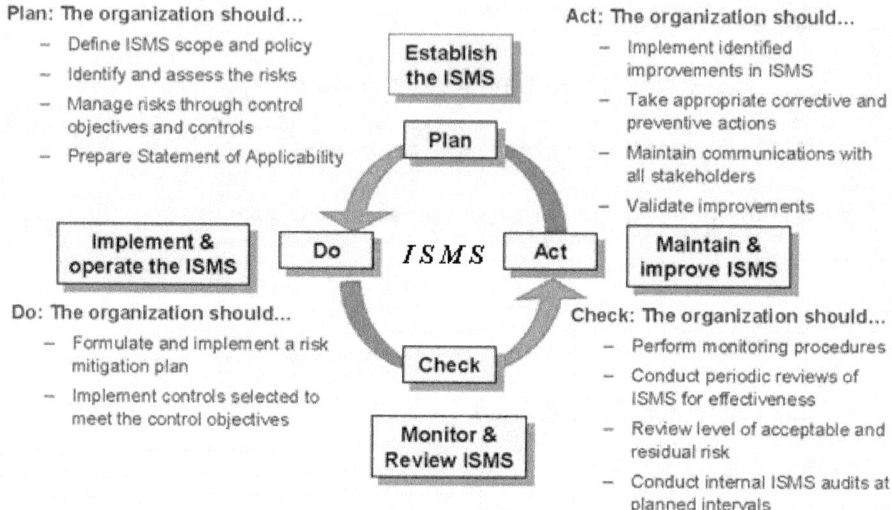

Conceptual Framework of ISMS

- The ISM process and framework will generally consist of:

  o An Information Security Policy and specific security policies that address each aspect of strategy, controls and regulation

  o An Information Security Management System (ISMS), containing the standards, management procedures and guidelines supporting the information security policies

  o A comprehensive security strategy, closely linked to the business objectives, strategies and plans

  o An effective security organizational structure

  o A set of security controls to support the policy

  o The management of security risks

Monitoring processes to ensure compliance and provide feedback on effectiveness

o   Communications strategy and plan for security

o   Training and awareness strategy and plan

The framework or the ISMS in turn provides a basis for the development of a cost-effective information security program that supports the business objectives:

o   It will involve the four Ps; people, process, products, partners

o   ISO 27001 is a formal standard against which organizations may seek independent certification

o   The ISMS shown in Figure 4.26 shows an approach that is widely used and is based on ISO 27001 among other recognized guidance.

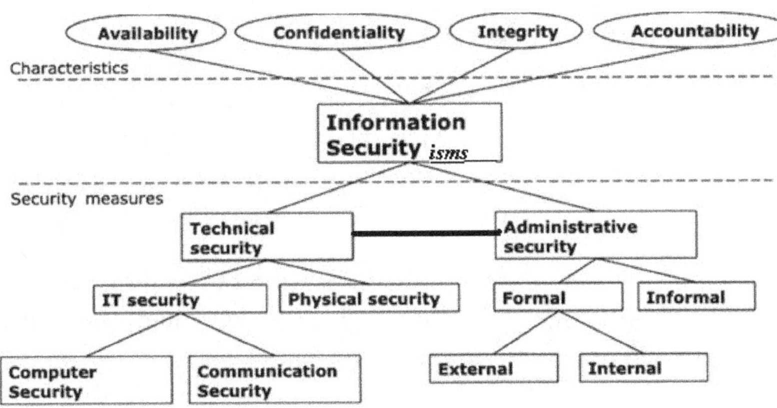

The five elements within this framework are:

1. Control

- The objective of control is to:

    - Establish a management framework to initiate and manage information security in the organization

    - Establish an organization structure to prepare, approve and implement the Information Security Policy

    - Allocate responsibilities

    - Establish and control documentation

2. Plan

- The objective of plan is to devise and recommend the appropriate security measures, based on an understanding of the requirements of the organization

- The Information Security Policy defines the organization's attitude and stance on security matters

3. Implement

- The objective of implement is to ensure that appropriate procedures, tools, and controls are in place to underpin the Information Security Policy

- Amongst the measures are:

- Accountability for assets

- Information Classification

- The successful implementation of the security controls and measures is dependent on a number of factors:

    - The determination of a clear and agreed policy, integrated with the needs of the business

    - Security procedures that are justified, appropriate and supported by senior management

    - Effective marketing and education in security requirements

    - A mechanism for improvement

4. Evaluation

- The objective of evaluation is to:

    - Supervise and check compliance with the security policy and security requirements in SLAs and OLAs

    - Carry out regular audits of the technical security of IT systems

    - Provide information to external auditors and regulators, if required

    -

5. Maintain

- The objective of maintain is to:

    - Improve security agreements as specified in, for example, SLAs and OLAs

    - Improve the implementation of security measures and controls-

        - This should be done with the PDCA cycle

        - Formal approach of ISO 27001

Steps for Developing ISMS

Developing ISMS involves many steps. While performing each step, inputs from all the stakeholders identified above should be included and results discussed to reach an agreed upon path. A security manual serves as the central repository for ISMS. This manual will be maintained by the Chief security officer and usually considered a confidential document. The various steps involved in building an ISMS are:

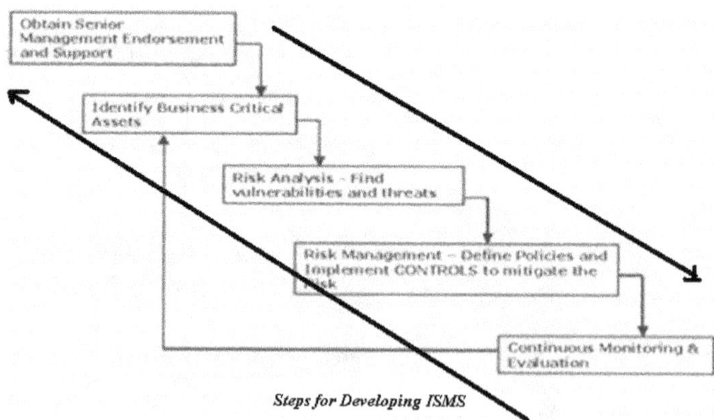

Steps for Developing ISMS

Step – 1: Risk Assessment

An industry accepted security risk assessment should be done. The goal is to identify assets, threats, vulnerabilities and controls to mitigate risks. Some risks will be accepted and management approval should be attained on this.

Step – 2: Top down approach

Security is a management issue and not just an IT issue. Hence it is critical that top management plays an important role in building ISMS. Management should have the overall ownership of ISMS. Management should encourage a culture within the enterprise to follow security principles.

Step – 3: Functional roles

Once management's approval is attained, functional roles will have to be identified. Depending on the type and size of the enterprise, the roles can vary in type and number. A chief information security officer should be identified who solely owns the ISMS. Other functional roles could include Data stewards, Security awareness trainers etc.

Step - 4: Write the Policy

The security policy is a document that states the enterprise's information security strategy at a high-level. The language in the policy is derived from the risk assessment. Details should be avoided in policy. In order to make the policy acceptable to all stakeholders, the wording in the policy should be at high level and align nicely with the enterprise's business priorities and goals.

Step – 4: Write the Standards

Standards are definite requirements that an enterprise should put forth for everybody to follow. The standards should support the security policy and be measurable. It is good practice to document what the penalties are when standards are not met

Step – 5: Write the guidelines and procedures

Guidelines are recommended ideas for an enterprise. They can also be termed as 'nice to haves'. It should be noted that the effectiveness of an enterprise's security management will not be measured by the guidelines present. There, usually, are no penalties for not following the guidelines. However, there can be some incentives if the enterprise follows the guidelines. Procedures are step by step description on how to meet the standards or guidelines so that the policy is supported. Procedures are usually targeted at the system level people who actually implement the control.

Designing ISMS:

The first step in designing an ISMS is to select the framework within which the ISMS will function. The framework will depend on the type of industry or the need to go for certification (such as BS7799)

Terminology

There should be a consistent use of terminologies in the entire ISMS infrastructure so that there is no room for confusion. In addition, the definitions to terminologies should be concise and clear. For example, a 'standard' is defined as requirement that supports the policy and can be measured, whereas a 'guideline' is defined as a best practice recommendation on how to meet requirements.

Authorization and ownership

Before starting to build and implement ISMS, all the stakeholders should be identified and the authorization agreed upon. Authorization exists in multiple levels such as authorization to adopt the policies, standards etc., authorization to change the policies, standards etc. There should also be documented authorization process in place.

The environment

It is always helpful to understand the environment and the space in which the enterprise is working in to effectively design ISMS. It is beneficial to know if the ISMS will ultimately satisfy a marketing requirement or a legal requirement for the enterprise. Some additional information on the environment that can be gathered could be:

- An org chart of the enterprise

- Is management centralized or decentralized?

Controls

The need for controls is an outcome of the risk assessment process. Once the need for controls is decided, the choice of control is done based on a cost-benefit analysis of the asset it is protecting and the control's cost itself. In ISMS, controls can be software, hardware, person or a process. In a good ISMS,they should be implemented and used for their intended purposes only.

Maintaining an ISMS

Everything in Information security should be an iterative process. ISMS is no different. An ISMS is built with a snapshot of information and may become outdated or obsolete, rendering the ISMS ineffective. A yearly audit of the ISMS is suggested. The audit should reveal the following:

- Are the controls online and performing their intended functions?

-Are there any new risks identified that need to be addressed?

-Do the policy, standards, guidelines and procedures need to be changed or updated?

-Identify gaps between what was set forth in the ISMS manual and what the practice is.

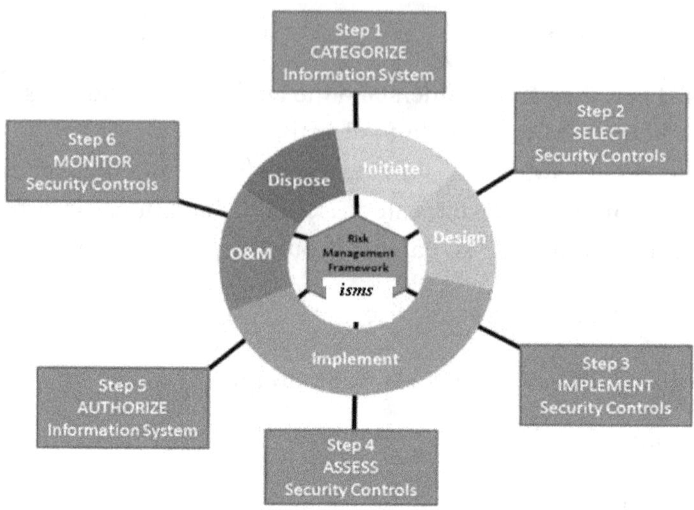

2.6 The 3 pillars CIA of Information Security:

Information security (InfoSec), as defined by the standards published by the Committee on National Security Systems (CNSS), formerly the National Security Telecommunications and Information Systems Security Committee (NSTISSC),is the protection of information and its critical elements, including the systems and hardware that use, store, and transmit that information. Information security includes the broad areas of information security management , computer and data security, and network security. To protect information and its related systems, organizations must implement such tools as policy, awareness, training and education, and technology. The NSTISSC model of information security evolved from a concept developed by the computer security industry known as the C.I.A. triangle.

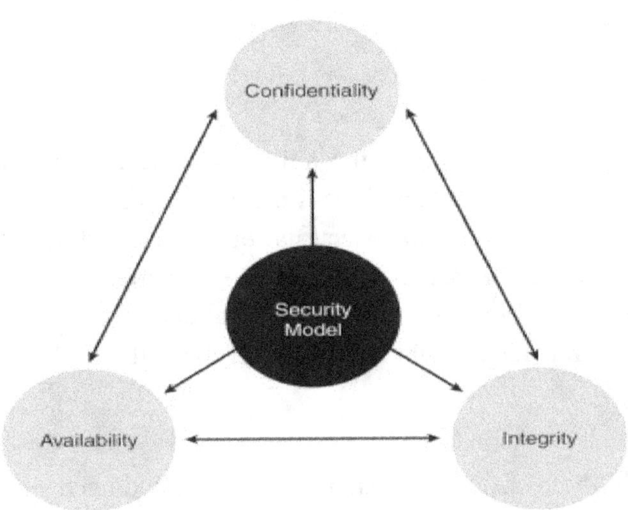

The **C.I.A.triangle** has been the industry standard for computer security since the development of the mainframe. It is based on the three characteristics of information that give it value for its use in organizations: confidentiality, integrity, and availability. The security of these three characteristics of information is as important today as it has always been, but the C.I.A. triangle model no longer adequately addresses the constantly changing environment of the computer industry. The threats to information confidentiality, integrity, and availability have evolved into a vast collection of events, including accidental or intentional damage, destruction, theft, unintended or unauthorized modification, or other misuses from human or nonhuman threats. This new environment of many constantly evolving threats has prompted the development of a more robust intellectual model .

The CIA principle

A simple but widely-applicable security model is the CIA triad; standing for Confidentiality, Integrity and Availability; three key principles which should be guaranteed in any kind of secure system. This principle is applicable across the whole subject of Security Analysis, from access to a user's internet history to security of encrypted data across the internet.

If any one of the three can be breached it can have serious consequences for the parties concerned.

1. Confidentiality:- Confidentiality is the ability to hide information from those people unauthorized to view it. It is perhaps the most obvious aspect of the CIA triad when it comes to security; but correspondingly, it is also the one which is attacked most often. Cryptography and Encryption methods are an example of an attempt to ensure confidentiality of data transferred from one computer to another.

2. Integrity:-The ability to ensure that data is an accurate and unchanged representation of the original secure information. One type of security attack is to intercept some important data and make changes to it before sending it on to the intended receiver.

3. Availability:-It is important to ensure that the information concerned is readily accessible to the authorized viewer at all times. Some types of security attack attempt to deny access to the appropriate user, either for the sake of inconveniencing them, or because there is some secondary effect. For example, by breaking the web site for a particular search engine, a rival may become more popular.

2.7 Information Classification:

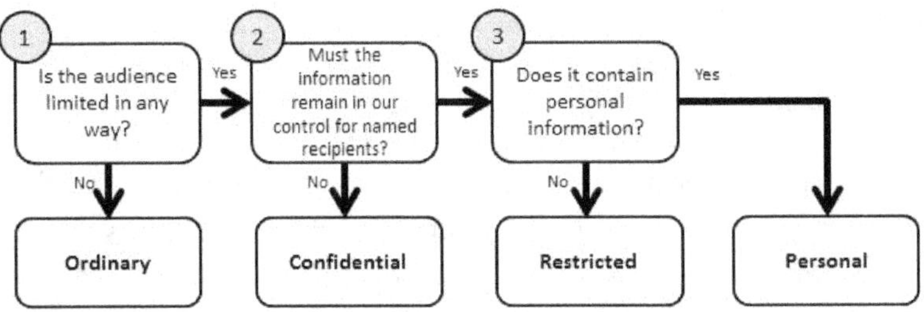

Classified information is material that a government body claims is sensitive information that requires protection of confidentiality, integrity, or availability. Access is restricted by law or regulation to articular groups of people, and mishandling can incur criminal penalties and loss of respect. A formal security clearance is often required to handle classified documents or access classified data. The clearance process usually requires a satisfactory background investigation. Documents and other information assets are typically marked with one of several (hierarchical) levels of sensitivity—e.g. restricted, confidential, secret and top secret. The choice of level is often based on an impact assessment; governments often have their own set of rules which include the levels, rules on determining the level for an information asset, and rules on how to protect information classified at each level. This often includes security clearances for personnel handling the information. Although "classified information" refers to the formal categorization and marking of material by level of sensitivity, it has also developed a sense synonymous with "censored" in US English. A distinction is often made between formal security classification and privacy markings such as "commercial in confidence".

Information Classification Definitions:

The following table provides a summary of the information classification levels that have been adopted by LSE and which underpin the 8 principles of information s security defined in the Information Security Policy (Section 3.1). These classification levels explicitly incorporate the Data Protection Act's (DPA) definitions of Personal Data and Sensitive Personal Data, as laid out in LSE's Data Protection Policy, and are designed to cover both primary and secondary research data.

1. Confidential

'Confidential' information has significant value for LSE, and unauthorized disclosure or dissemination could result in severe financial or reputational damage to LSE, including fines of up to £500,000 from the Information Commissioner's Office, the revocation of research contracts and the failure to win future research bids. Data that is defined by the Data Protection Act as Sensitive Personal Data falls into this category. Only those who need explicitly need access must be granted it, and only to the least degree in order to do their work (the 'need to know' and 'least privilege' principles). When held outside LSE, on mobile devices such as laptops, tablets or phones, or in transit, 'Confidential' information must be protected behind an explicit logon and by AES 256-bit encryption at the device, drive or file level.

2. Restricted

'Restricted' information is subject to controls on access, such as only allowing valid logons from a small

group of staff. 'Restricted' information must be held in such a manner that prevents unauthorized access i.e. on a system that requires a valid and appropriate user to log in before access is granted. Information defined as Personal Data by the Data Protection Act falls into this category. Disclosure or dissemination of this information is not intended, and may incur some negative publicity, but is unlikely

to cause severe financial or reputational damage to LSE. Note that under the Data Protection Act large datasets (>1000 records) of 'Restricted' information may become classified as Confidential, thereby requiring a higher level of access control.

3. Internal Use

'Internal use' information can be disclosed or disseminated by its owner to appropriate members Of LSE, partners and other individuals, as appropriate by information owners without any restrictions on content or time of publication.

4. Public

'Public' information can be disclosed or disseminated without any restrictions on content, audience or time of publication. Disclosure or dissemination of the information must not violate any applicable laws or regulations, such as privacy rules. Modification must be restricted to individuals who have been explicitly approved by information owners to modify that Information, and who have successfully.

Authenticated them to the appropriate computer system. Designating information as 'Confidential' involves significant costs in terms of implementation, hardware and ongoing resources, and makes data less mobile. For this reason, information owners making classification decisions must balance the risk of damage that could result from unauthorized access to, or disclosure of, the information against the cost of additional hardware, software or services required to protect it.

2.8 Risk Analysis & Management:

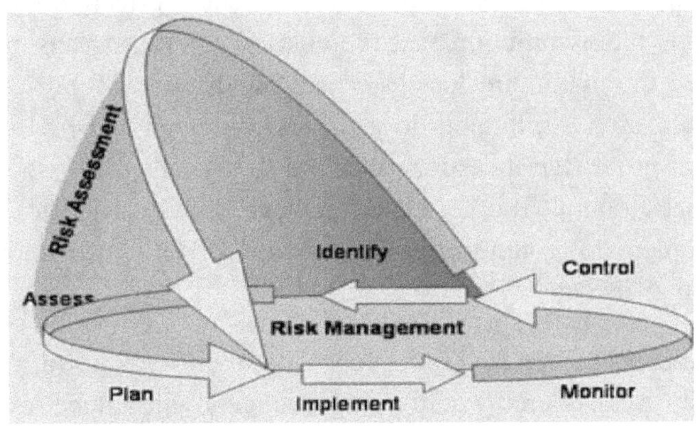

Information security analysts are information technology (IT) specialists who are accountable for safeguarding all data and communications that are stored and shared in network systems. In the financial industry, for example, information security analysts might continually upgrade firewalls that prohibit superfluous access to sensitive business data and might perform defenselessness tests to assess the effectiveness of security measures.

Risk Analysis helps establish a good security posture; Risk Management keeps it that way. Security measures cannot assure 100% protection against all threats. Therefore, risk analysis, which is the process of evaluating system vulnerabilities and the threats facing it, is an essential part of any risk management program. The analysis process identifies the probable consequences or risks associated with the vulnerabilities and provide the basis for establishing a cost-effective security program. Risk management is the process of implementing and maintaining countermeasures that reduce the effects of risk to an acceptable level. The risk analysis process gives management the information it needs to make educated judgments concerning information security. The procedure identifies the existing

Security controls, calculates vulnerabilities, and evaluates the effect of threats on each area of vulnerability. In most cases, the risk analysis procedure attempts to strike an economic balance

Between the impact of risks and the cost of security solutions intended to manage them. At the basis of selecting cost -effective protective e measures is the assumption that the cost of controlling any risk should not exceed the maximum loss associated with the risk. For example, if the potential loss attributable to a risk is estimated to be $100,000, the cost of the protective measures intended to prevent that loss should not exceed that amount. In other cases, however, the decision to implement (or not implement) countermeasures may be driven by the importance of the system or its data

Or by mandates as opposed to its cost. In either case, the sum of averted risks must be considered where a single remedy will reduce several risks. The analyst must also consider the use and interaction of multiple remedies. One remedy may improve or negate the effectiveness of another

The risk management steps include:

• Assign and track corrective actions, as necessary, to reduce residual risk to an acceptable level.

• Continuously monitor the security posture a security risk analysis is a procedure for estimating the risk to computer related assets and loss because of manifested threats. The procedure first determines an asset's level of vulnerability by identifying and evaluating the effect of in -place countermeasures.

An asset's level of vulnerability to the threat population is determined solely by countermeasures [controls/safeguards] that are in -place at the time the risk analysis is done. Next, detailed info

- ✓ Risk Analysis Terminology
- ✓ Asset
  - Anything with value and in need of protection.
- ✓ Threat
  - An action or potential action with the propensity to cause damage.
- ✓ Vulnerability
  - A condition of weakness.

If there were no vulnerabilities, there would be no concern for threat activity.

Countermeasure

- Any device or action with the ability to reduce vulnerability.

Expected Loss

- The anticipated negative impact to assets due to threat manifestation.

Impact

- Losses as a result of threat activity are normally expressed in one or more impact areas. Four areas are commonly used; Destruction, Denial of Service, Disclosure, and Modification.

How

IT risk management is the application of risk management methods to information technology in order to manage IT risk, i.e.:

The business risk associated with the use, ownership, operation, involvement, influence and adoption of IT within an enterprise or organization

IT risk management can be considered a component of a wider enterprise risk management system.[1] (Fiscal)

The establishment, maintenance and continuous update of an ISMS provide a strong indication that a company is using a systematic approach for the identification, assessment and management of information security risk.

Different methodologies have been proposed to manage IT risks, each of them divided in processes and steps.[3]

According to Risk IT it encompasses not just only the negative impact of operations and service delivery which can bring destruction or reduction of the value of the organization, but also the benefit\value enabling risk associated to missing opportunities to use technology to enable or enhance business or the IT project management for aspects like overspending or late delivery with adverse business impact.

Because risk is strictly tied to uncertain

Risk management constituent processes			
ISO/IEC 27005:2008	**BS 7799-3:2006**	**SP 800-30**	**Risk IT**
Context establishment	Organizational context		RG and RE Domains more precisely • RG1.2 Propose IT risk tolerance, • RG2.1 Establish and maintain accountability for IT risk management • RG2.3 Adapt IT risk practices to enterprise risk practices, • RG2.4 Provide adequate resources for IT risk management, • RE2.1 Define IT risk analysis scope.
Risk assessment	Risk assessment	Risk assessment	RE2 process includes: • RE2.1 Define IT risk analysis scope. • RE2.2 Estimate IT risk.

			• RE2.3 Identify risk response options. • RE2.4 Perform a peer review of IT risk analysis. In general, the elements as described in the ISO 27005 process are all included in Risk IT; however, some are structured and named differently.
Risk treatment	Risk treatment and management decision making	Risk mitigation	• RE 2.3 Identify risk response options • RR2.3 Respond to discovered risk exposure and opportunity
Risk acceptance			RG3.4 Accept IT risk
Risk communication	Ongoing risk management activities		• RG1.5 Promote IT risk-aware culture • RG1.6 Encourage effective communication of IT risk • RE3.6 Develop IT risk indicators.

Risk monitoring and review		Evaluation and assessment	<ul><li>RG2 Integrate with ERM.</li><li>RE2.4 Perform a peer review of IT risk analysis.</li><li>RG2.5 Provide independent assurance over IT risk management</li></ul>

Due to the probabilistic nature and the need of cost benefit analysis,

the IT risks are managed following a process that accordingly to

1. risk assessment,

2. risk mitigation, and

3. Evaluation and assessment.

Risk Analysis Framework

The HIPAA Security Rule does not require a specific methodology or process for conducting a risk analysis. However, it does reference the National Institute of Standards and Technology (NIST) Special Publication (SP) 800-30, Risk Management Guide for Information Technology Systems. This publication provides a comprehensive framework that both the Department of Health and Human Services (HHS) and CMS reference in the following publications:

- The HIPAA Security Rule[4]

- 6 Basics of Risk Analysis and Risk Management[5]

- HIPAA Compliance Review Analysis and Summary of Results[6]

- Guidance on Risk Analysis Requirements under the HIPAA Security Rule[7]

The original NIST SP 800-30 was retired and replaced with the following publications:

- 800-30 Guide for Conducting Risk Assessments, Revision 1 (September 2012)

- 800-39 Managing Information Security Risk: Organization, Mission, and Information System View (March 2011)

Note: Because this practice brief is intended to provide a high-level overview, AHIMA recommends that the reader download NIST SPs 800-30 and 800-39 for a more detailed explanation of risk analysis.

Step 1. System Characterization

System characterization is the process of identifying the information assets that require a risk analysis. The information assets require protection either because of their criticality to the business and/or because the systems process and store phi. System characterization requires an inventory of major applications and general support systems—that is, any systems that process or store PHI. A major application is one that is critical to an organization or that stores PHI. Generally, the 'owner' of a major application is the director of the department that primarily uses that application. Following are some examples of major applications and their probable owners:

- Electronic health record (EHR) [chief operating officer and/or chief information officer]

- Laboratory information system [director of laboratory]

- Pharmacy system—medication dispensing carts [director of pharmacy]

General support systems are the systems used throughout the organization to support one or more applications. They are usually 'owned' by the information technology (IT) department. Following are some examples of general support systems:

- Computer workstations

- Laptops and tablets

- Smartphones and other mobile devices

- Network (wired and wireless)

- E-mail system

An organization's risk analysis should initially focus on systems that have the greatest effect on healthcare operations as well as systems that pose the greatest risk for the organization. A business impact analysis, often conducted before creating a disaster recovery plan, is one method used to determine information system criticality.

Another method for identifying the systems on which the healthcare organization should focus is to rank applications systems based on risk factors, such as:

- Number of users (i.e., the greater the number of users, the higher the risk)

- Type of information (i.e., the more sensitive the information, the higher the risk – Social Security Numbers, HIV data, bank account numbers, credit card data, etc.),

- Use of the information (i.e., patient care, research, business intelligence, patient accounting, etc.)

- Availability of the information (e.g., hosted in the cloud via the Internet, standalone system, virtualized servers, mirrored SAN, etc.)

- Mobility of the information (i.e., the more mobile, the greater the risk – portable media, smartphone, tablet, laptop, etc.)

- Effects on the organization and patients if the system is not available

- Other factors that might indicate that a system has a higher relative risk for the organization (i.e., system frequently goes down, system provide interconnectivity to other applications and system such as an interface engine, etc.

A risk analysis can be time-consuming. Therefore, healthcare organizations should initially focus should be on the 'critical few' versus the 'trivial many.' However, all applications and systems (including biomedical devices) containing phi must eventually be assessed.

Step 2. Threat Identification

Once major applications and general support systems have been categorized, the next step is to identify threats. From an information security perspective, a threat is anything that could affect the confidentiality, integrity, or availability of information or an information system.

There are three types of threats:

- **Acts of nature** (e.g., lightning, earthquakes, hurricanes, and tornadoes)

- **Acts of humans** (e.g., carelessness, human errors, unauthorized access, identity theft; tampering; hacking into data; and theft of equipment by internal workforce members, external hackers, and visitors)

- **Environmental** (e.g., hardware failure, power outage, inoperable air conditioning that leads to overheating, break in the network cable, and water leaking from the ceiling)

Conducting a thorough risk analysis does not imply that organizations must identify every possible threat. The term "reasonably anticipated" is used three times within the HIPAA security rule (twice in the preamble and once in the actual rule) as it pertains to threats or hazards. Instead, they should consider these factors:

- Statistics (i.e. HHS website for reported breaches affecting over 500 patients)

- Geographical location (i.e. hurricane for coastal areas, tornado for the Midwest, volcano for Hawaii)

- Past experiences (i.e. incident reports indicate areas of vulnerability that have been exploited before – theft of equipment in public areas)

- Industry trends (i.e. surveys, reports, security alerts, patches or system updates)

Once identified, the reasonably anticipated threats are matched to a particular application or general support system. For example, the probability of theft is more likely for a laptop or a smartphone that is transported daily in and out of an organization. Alternatively, theft may not be a reasonably anticipated threat for a large rack-mounted server in a data center.

System characterization divides information assets into manageable pieces and helps healthcare organizations identify the unique threats that may exist at each layer of an information system, including the application, the operating system, any software, the server, the network, and desktop and laptop levels of use.

Steps 3 & 4.Control Assessment and Vulnerability Identification

Vulnerabilities and controls should go hand in hand, and it's often easier to combine the identification of both into one step. If a major application or general support system is already in use, then a healthcare organization should first conduct a control analysis. If an application or system is new and not currently active, then the healthcare organization should perform a vulnerability identification first because some of the security controls may not have been implemented fully yet.

A vulnerability is as an inherent weakness or absence of a safeguard that a threat could exploit. Vulnerabilities may be attributed to people, processes, or technologies. The absence of a functioning control often represents vulnerability in an application or system. For example, antivirus software is used to prevent or detect malicious code. If this control is missing, it represents vulnerability. Sometimes a control may be present but inadequate. Using the same example, if the antivirus software is present but does not get updated regularly, this is also vulnerability.

Typically, threats are correlated with vulnerabilities, although it is not necessarily a one-to-one relationship. Many threats may exploit a single vulnerability. One threat source may exploit more than one vulnerability. Conversely, a single control may be used to address multiple threats. Figure 2, offers samples of controls and vulnerabilities based on a specific threat for laptops.

Sample of Threats, Controls, and Vulnerabilities

Threat	Control	Vulnerability
1. Theft or loss	File encryption is used to protect some of the data stored on the hard drive.	Power-on passwords and other access control devices are not being used. Security devices (physical or technical) for tracking lost or stolen laptops are lacking.
2. Malicious code (e.g., virus, worm, Trojan horse, spyware)	Antivirus software is loaded on laptops.	Antivirus software does not get updated regularly. Users have local administrator rights and can disable or turn off the antivirus software and download executable programs.

In general, controls may be categorized as:

- **Preventive**—Inhibiting a threat, such as access controls, encryption, and authentication requirements

- **Deterrent**—Keeping the casual threat away, such as strong passwords, two-tiered authentication, and Internet use policies

- **Detective**—Identifying and proving when a threat has occurred or is about to occur, such as audit trails, intrusion detection, and checksums

- **Reactive**—Providing a means to respond to a threat that has occurred, such as an alarm or penetration test

- **Recovery**—A control that helps retrieve or recreate data or applications, such as backup systems and contingency plans

In addition to control analysis, other sources for determining vulnerabilities include reports or results from:

- Past incidents or data breaches, including news stories about reported data breaches at other organizations

- Audits or evaluations conducted by external or internal auditors

- A compliance gap analysis or privacy and security assessment

- Patient complaints to determine whether a breakdown or flaw in a security control exists

- A walk-through inspection (e.g., workstations being left unattended while logged on to an information system containing confidential information)

- A network vulnerability scanning or penetration test

Web sites, such as the HHS Web site, that post breaches[8] affecting more than 500 individuals

3. Information Security Models, Frameworks, Standards & Legal Framework

3.1 A structure and framework of compressive security policy

3.2 policy infrastructure

3.3 policy design life cycle and design processes

3.4 PDCA model

3.5 Security policy standards and practices -ISO 27001, SSECMM, IA-CMM, ITIL & BS 15000 BS7799

3.6 Understanding Laws for Information Security

3.7 Legislative Solutions

3.8 Contractual Solutions

3.9 Evidential Issues

3.10 International Activity Indian IT Act

3.11 Laws of IPR Indian

3.12 Copyright Act

3.1 A structure and framework of compressive security policy:

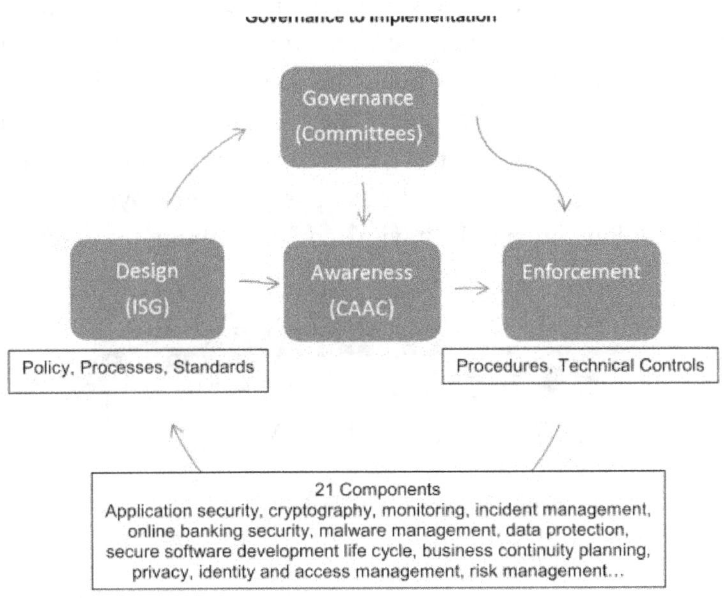

Types of Information Security Policies- Administrative and Technical

There are different types of policies in an organization, such as HR Policies, Finance Policies, IT Policies, Information Security Policies and Information Management Policies.

- **"HR policies"** focus on issues such as leave, safety and health, smoking, sexual harassment and HIV/AIDS

- **"Information security policies"** focus on managing and protecting and preserving data belonging to the organization which is generated by those employees in the course and scope of their employment;

- **"IT policies"** are closely related to "information security policies", but focus on the supporting processes (e.g. procurement policies) and supporting systems;

- **"Information Management policies"** focus managing data such as its retention and destruction.

There is an overlap between HR policies and information security policies to the extent that the "human factor" is common to both of them and both therefore cover issues involved in the employer and employee relationship. In our experience, the HR and IT Departments are not good at "speaking to one another" the end result being that a lot of important information security related risks posed by employees through their use of technology are not dealt with and "fall through the cracks".

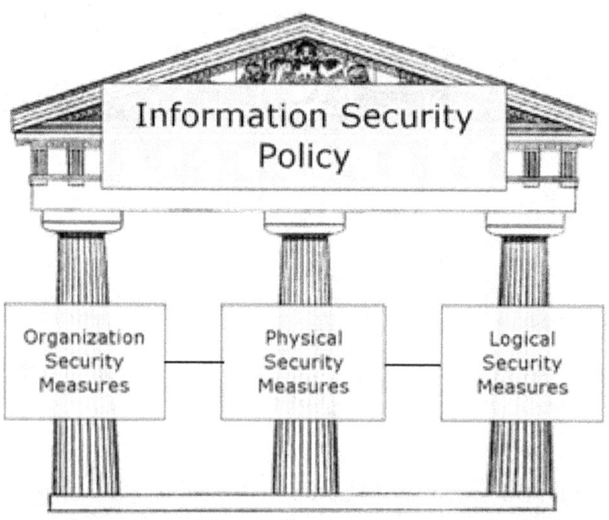

Different companies will need different policies for effective security management. Below is a list of standard policies that would make up an organization's security policy. Some companies may need all these policies, while others need only a handful. That said, certain policies can reasonably considered "essential" to security management and are applicable to most every company. These are denoted below with an asterisk.

1. Acceptable Use Policy
2. Authentication Policy
3. Data Classification Policy
4. Incident Response Policy
5. Mobile Device Policy
6. Backup Policy
7. Confidential Data Policy
8. Network Access Policy
9. Encryption Policy
10. Remote Access Policy
11. Retention Policy
12. Third Party Connection Policy
13. Email Policy
14. Guest Access Policy
15. Network Security policy
16. Outsourcing Policy
17. Password Policy
18. Physical Security policy
19. VPN Policy

As part of our information security service offering, we draft or review information security policies in accordance with our **"Information Security Policy Framework"**.

These are some of the more important and essential policies are:

1. Access control

2. Acceptable usage

3. E-mail usage

4. Incident response

5. Internet usage

6. Mobile technology

7. Bring your own device (BYOD)

8. Computer usage

9. Monitoring

10. Social media.

11. Physical and environmental

We advocate an approach which clearly differentiates between issue specific, operational policies, standards and procedures, each of which should be set forth in separate documents. However, certain client specifically wants one policy that covers several areas that we normally cover in separate policies. For them we have developed an **"Electronic Communications Policy (ECP)"**.

Structure and Framework of Compressive Security Policy

An IT security policy framework contains main 4 components:-

Policy: - A policy is a short defined statement that the in charge of an organization has set as a course of action of direction; Policy comes from top management and applies to entire organization.

Standard: - A standard is detailed written definition for software and hardware and how it is to be used. Standard ensure that consistent security controls are used throughout the IT system.

Procedure: - These are written instructions for how to use policies and standards. They may include a plan of action, testing, installation and auditing of security controls

Guidelines: - A guidelines is a suggested course of action for using the policy. Standards, procedure, guidelines can be specific or flexible regarding use.

An IT Security framework is the foundation for an effective, enterprise wide security programas adopted the International Standards Organization' s (ISO) Information Security Framework documented as ISO 27001 and 27002.This framework outlines many actions and controls needed to ensure the organizations appropriately protects the information assets it owns and creates.

The Security framework is a code of practice and principles that includes process, policy and procedures used here in organization that protect and govern information security. The framework is a method of establishing, implementing, reviewing, maintaining and improving the security programs throughout the university community.

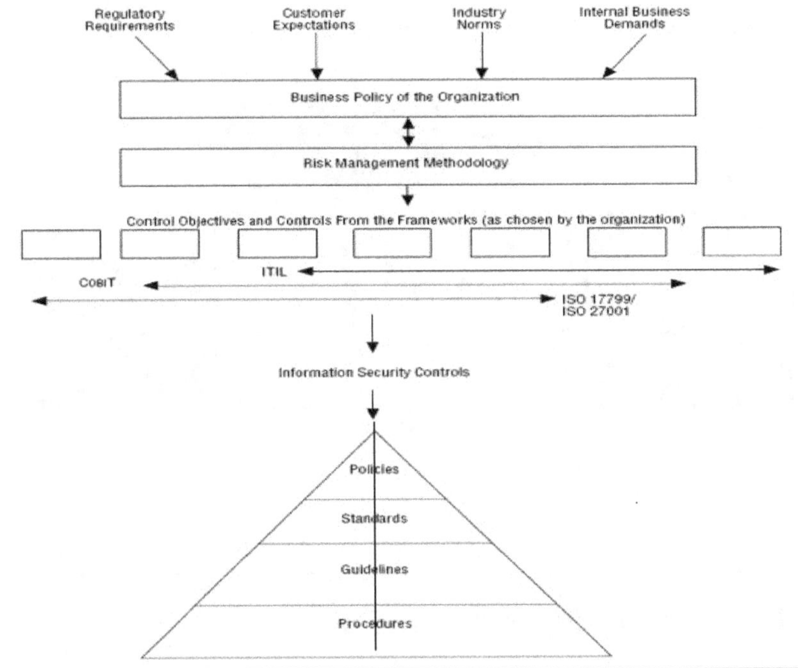

The implementation of the Security Framework is a multi-year project. Completing the initial work for implementing the various controls required to address information security concerns across an organizations varies as work must be parceled and planned to make the most gains using allocated resources.

3.2 Policy Infrastructure:

The information security infrastructure comprises the individuals, groupings, communication channels and physical resources involved in developing, maintaining and implementing an information security policy. In a university or college setting this will encompass officers with specific responsibilities for devising, maintaining and publicizing the policy, committees at various levels endorsing and promulgating the policy and the websites, documents and other communication channels necessary to bring the relevant parts of the Information Security Policy to the attention of the organization's staff, students, suppliers, contractors and the external agencies and individuals with which it interacts. Where appropriate, the infrastructure should also enable communications with external authorities and specialist groups.

3.3 Policy Design Life Cycle:

The essence of an IT security policy is to establish guidelines and standards for accessing the organizations information and application systems. As IT infrastructures have become more complex and organizations resources have become more distributed, the need for improved information security has increased.

An IT security policy facilitates the communication of security procedures to users and makes them more aware of potential security threats and associated business risks. A written IT security policy helps to enhance the performance of the organizations IT security systems and the e-business systems that they support.

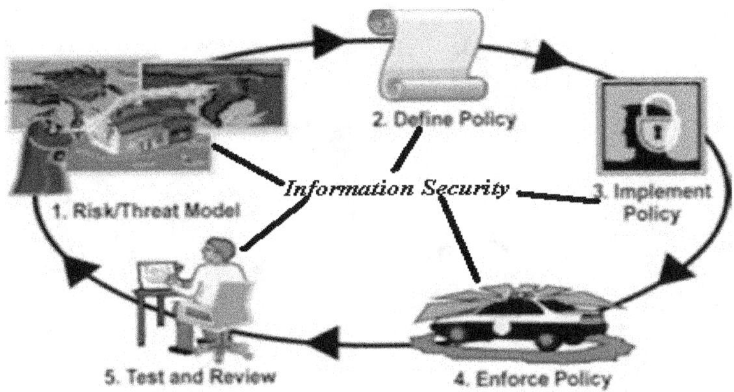

An IT security policy mitigates the organizations legal exposure. The security policy guides the behavior of employees. Having a written IT security policy is essential if the organization wants to be able to hold employees accountable for their actions.

An IT security policy forces an organization to make return on investment decisions. Whilst, developing an IT security policy the organization will have to make intelligent business decisions about the cost-effectiveness of reducing or eliminating business risks.

If an organist ion suffers an IT security breach it is likely to suffer negative impact. There are many costs associated with a security breach:

- direct financial loss,

- lost sales and reduced competitive advantage,

- damage to organization reputation and brand,

- Business disruption.

Developing and IT Security Policy

To develop and IT security policy a task force needs to be established and the task force will need to work through the following steps:

- Access the requirements,

- Identify the information assets, systems and facilities,

- Implement the security policy,

- Communicate the security policy,

- Enforce the security policy,

- Identify the threats to the assets,

- Assess the risks to the assets,

- Develop an security policy to manage the risks,

- Re-assess the security policy,

IT Security Policy Contents - The IT security policy should deal with security threats to the organizations information assets with respect to the following fundamental areas:

- Authentication - ensuring a user is who he says he is,

- Authorization - controlling what information and applications a user can access,

- Privacy and data integrity - preventing unauthorized users from seeing certain information, and preventing them from making unauthorized changes or deletions,

- Non-repudiation - making sure that parties in a transaction cannot deny what they said or what they did,

- Disaster recovery and contingency planning,

- Physical security.

The IT security policy should have sections dealing with the following issues:

- Access control

- Electronic Mail

- Internet security

- Laptops, notebooks and handhelds

- Software security

- Network security

- Physical security

- Auditing and monitoring

- Contingency planning

Implementing the IT Security Policy -Once the IT security policy has is written it needs to be put in place within the organization. It needs to be communicated to employees, contractors and other personnel to ensure that they understand the security policy and what is required.

The IT security policy will then need to be enforced. IT and security staff will need to implement its contents. They will need to manage user accounts, passwords, group membership, two-factor authentication devices such as smartcards and digital certificates.

The rapid pace of technological change and use of the Internet mean that new security threats appear all the time. The IT security policy will therefore need updating on a periodic basis.

IT Security Policy Summary -An IT security policy is a formal statement of the rules that employees and others must follow when using an organizations IT infrastructure. Its purpose is to set down procedures for protecting the organizations information assets. AnIT security policy which details a number of security procedures to minimize business risk is available below.

Design Processes

Security design process, that the process is cyclical. The rationale for this is quite simple: threats, both business and technical, change rapidly, and it's important that you stay on top of old and new threats to your applications and understand their security implications.

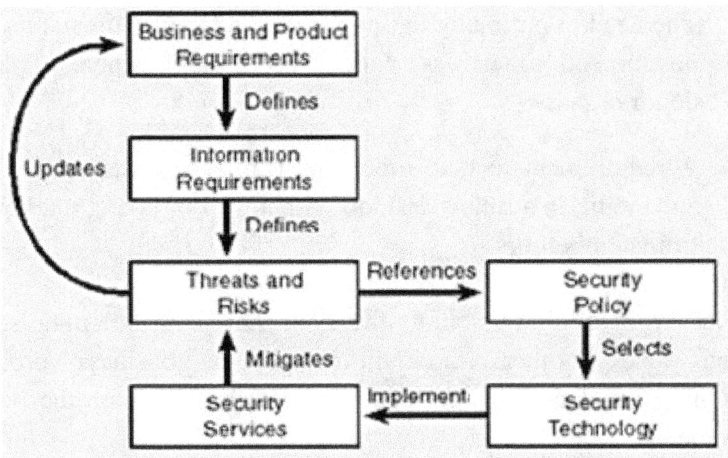

As you can see, the process begins with business and product requirements: the details of what you want your business and its tools to be able to do. The process has no room for the notion of technology for technology's sake. You must choose technology because it's the right tool for the job, not because it happens to be the technology.

Note also how much of the process involves information gathering and decision making prior to any actual development work. Only at the last step—indicated by the Security Services box—does the nuts-and-bolts development begin. The process comprises a lot of research and planning to help ensure that the solution you ultimately build is the best response to your security needs.

Examples of high-level business requirements include the following:

- The ability to provide insurance information to field personnel quickly and effectively—most notably, the capacity to create insurance quotes for clients within five minutes of gathering all requisite client data

- The capability to determine the most cost-effective combination of goods and shipping methods based on quantity, shipping schedules, special offers, and previous sales history

- The need to optimally define medical operation timetables based on surgeon timetables, patient needs, and, where applicable, donor organs

- A requirement to take orders from clients, based on inventory and credit, in a timely fashion with a goal of taking market share from competitors

Now let's turn our attention to the next step in developing security solutions and another important aspect of business processes: determining the data and information required to back up the business requirements.

A good IT policy must be based on the results of a local survey and risk assessment. Findings your use of IT resources and doing a risk assessment provide policy-makers with an accurate picture of the security needs specific to your organization. This information is imperative because proper policy development requires decision-makers to:

- Identify sensitive information and critical systems

- Incorporate local, state, and federal laws, as well as relevant ethical standards

- Define institutional security goals and objectives

- Set a course for accomplishing those goals and objectives

- Ensure that necessary mechanisms for accomplishing the goals and objectives are in place

The final step of the security design process is designing security services that use security technologies. The purpose of security services is to mitigate all risks to a tolerable level. Any security service that does not mitigate one or more risks should not be built; if the service doesn't counter a threat, there's no reason to build it.

3.4 PDCA Model:

PDCA (plan–do–check–act) is an iterative four-step management method used in business for the control and continuous improvement of processes and products. It is also known as the Deming circle. ISMS must remain effective and efficient in the long term, adapting to changes in the internal organization and external environment. **ISO/IEC 27001:2005** therefore incorporated the **"Plan-Do-Check-Act"** (PDCA), or Deming cycle, approach:

- The **Plan** phase is about designing the ISMS, assessing information security risks and selecting appropriate controls.

- The **Do** phase involves implementing and operating the controls.

- The **Check** phase objective is to review and evaluate the performance (efficiency and effectiveness) of the ISMS.

- In the **Act** phase, changes are made where necessary to bring the ISMS back to peak performance.

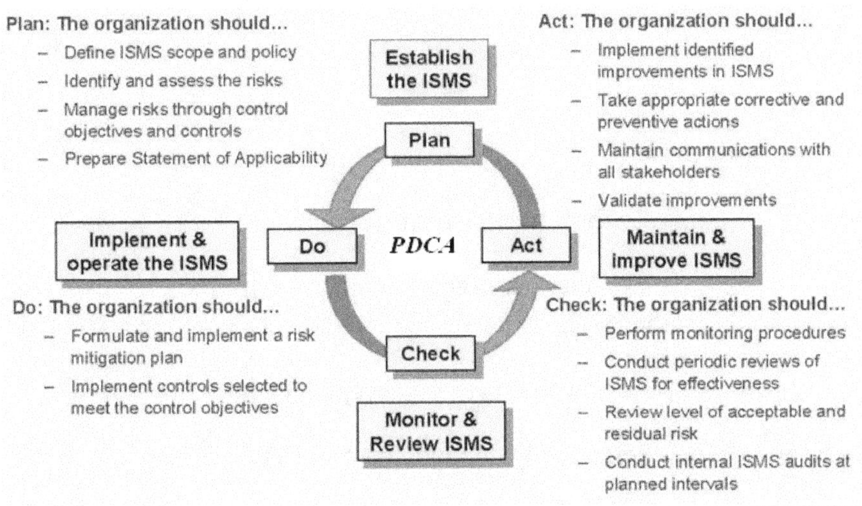

Plan

- Define the ISMS scope and the organization'ssecurity policies

- Identify and assess risks

- Select control objectives and controls that will helpmanage these risks

- Prepare the statement of applicability

Do

- Formulate and implement a risk mitigation plan

- Implement the previously selected controls in orderto meet the control objectives.

Check

- Perform monitoring procedures

- Conduct periodic reviews to verify the effectivenessof the ISMS

- Review the levels of acceptable and residual risk

- Periodically conduct internal ISMS audits

Act

- Implement identified ISMS improvements

- Take appropriate corrective and preventive action

- Maintain communications with all stakeholders

- Validate improvements

ISO/IEC 27001:2005 is a risk based information security standard, which means that organizations need to have a risk management process in place. The risk management process fits into the PDCA model given above. By the application of the **"Plan-Do-Check-Act (PDCA)"** model to processes associated with information security, the effect of information security satisfying "information security requirements and expectations of interested parties" can be produced through the processes as outputs, from those requirements and expectations put into it as inputs. The main point of the **JIS Q 27001(ISO/IEC 27001)** is the continual improvement of the processes that produce the effects by applying this PDCA model.

Plan **(Establish the ISMS)**	Establish ISMS policy, objectives, processes and procedures relevant to managing risk and improving information security to deliver results in accordance with an organization's overall policies and objectives.
Do **(Implement and operate the ISMS)**	Implement and operate the ISMS policy, controls, processes and procedures.
Check **(Monitor and review the ISMS)**	Assess and, where applicable, measure process performance against ISMS policy, objectives and practical experience and report the results to management for review.
Act **(Maintain and improve the**	Take corrective and preventive actions, based on the results of the internal ISMS audit and management review or other

ISMS)	relevant information, to achieve continual improvement of the ISMS.

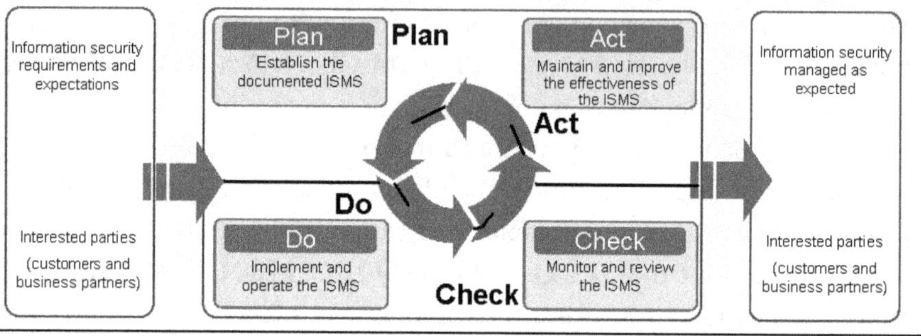

3.5 Security policy standards and practices -ISO 27001, SSECMM, IA-CMM, ITIL & BS 15000 BS7799:

Policy

Set of guidelines or instructions.

Regulates the activities of the organization members who make decisions, take actions, and perform other duties

Standards

- ✓ More detailed descriptions of what must be done to comply with policy
- ✓ Informal part of an organization's culture
- ✓ Published, scrutinized, and ratified by a group
- ✓ For a policy to be considered effective and legally enforceable:
- ✓ Dissemination (distribution)

- ✓ Review (reading)
- ✓ Comprehension (understanding)
- ✓ Compliance (agreement)
- ✓ Uniform enforcement
- ✓ Mission of an organization
- ✓ Written statement of purpose of organization
- ✓ Vision of an organization
- ✓ Witten statement of the organization's long-term goals
- ✓ Strategic planning
- ✓ Process of moving the organization toward its vision.
- ✓ Security policy
- ✓ Set of rules that protects an organization's assets
- ✓ Information security policy
- ✓ Set of rules for the protection of an organization's information assets
- ✓ Enterprise information security policies
- ✓ Issue-specific security policies
- ✓ Systems-specific security policies

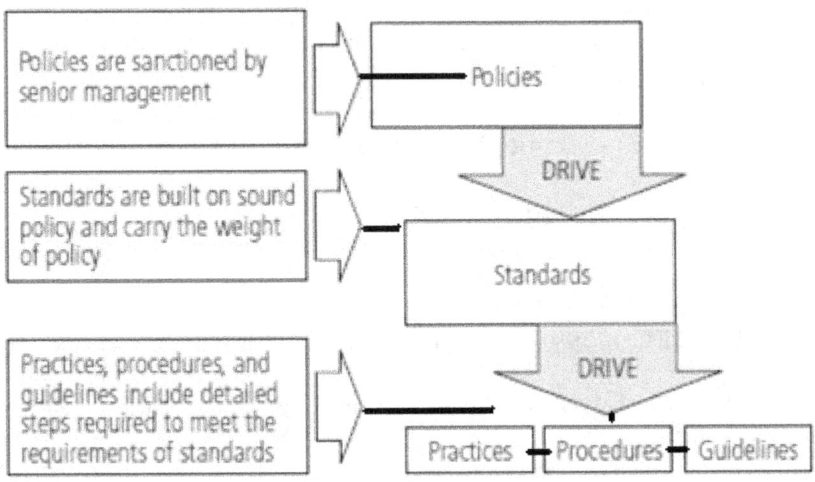

3.5.1 BS7799:

The essence of BS 7799 is that a sound Information Security Management System (ISMS) should be established within organizations. The purpose of this is to ensure that an organization's information is secure and properly managed.

BS 7799 is the most influential, globally recognized standard for information security management. BS 7799 Part 1 became an international standard (ISO/IEC 17799) in December 2000. It has recently been revised in line with ISO procedures and the revised standard should be available during 2005. BS 7799 Part 2, although still a UK standard, has been published as a national standard in many countries and is now itself at an advanced stage of the process towards international status. It is expected that this process will be complete by late 2005.

The standard is currently divided into two parts:

Part 1. Contains guidance and explanatory information

Part 2. Provides a model that can be used by businesses to set up and run an effective

Information Security Management System (ISMS)

The two parts are currently published as:

ISO/IEC 17799 Code of Practice for Information Security

BS 7799-2:2002 Specification for Information Security Management

---

Benefits of Using BS 7799 -The benefits of using ISO/IEC 17799 are straightforward. Using it well will result in:

- Reduced operational risk

- Increased business efficiency

- Assurance that information security is being rationally applied

This is achieved by ensuring that:

- Security controls are justified

- Policies and procedures are appropriate

- Security awareness is good amongst staff and managers

- All security relevant information processing and supporting activities are auditable and are being audited

- Internal audit, incident reporting / management mechanisms are being treated appropriately

- Management actively focus on information security and its effectiveness

It is likely that a number of organizations, including Government, will require suppliers and other partners to be certified to BS 7799 before they can be given work. This could make compliance (or certification) more of a necessity than a benefit.

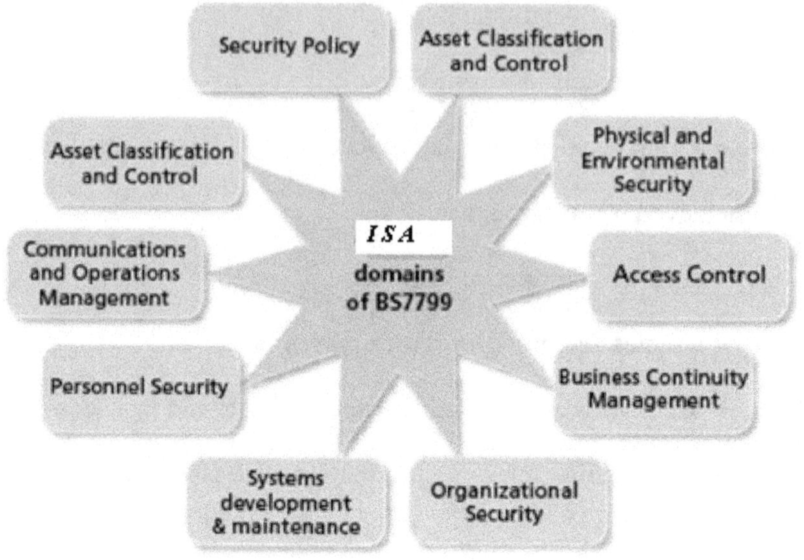

Ten Steps in BS7799

1. Security Policy - explains what an information security policy should coverand why each business should have one

2. Organizational Security – explains how information security managementis organized

3. Asset Classification and Control – considers information and informationprocessing equipment as valuable assets to be managed and accounted for

4. Personnel Security – details any personnel issues such as training, responsibilities, vetting procedures, and how staff responded tosecurity incidents

5. Physical and Environmental Security – physical aspects of securityincluding protection of equipment and information from physical harm, as well as physical control of access to information and equipment

6. Communications and Operations Management – examines correctmanagement and secure operation of information processing facilitiesduring day-to-day activities

7. Access Control – control of access to information and systems on thebasis of business and security needs

8. System Development and Maintenance – design and maintenance ofsystems so that they are secure and maintain information integrity

9. Business Continuity Management – concerns the maintenance ofessential business activities during adverse conditions, from copingwith major disasters to minor, local issues

10. Compliance – concerns business compliance with relevant national andinternational laws, professional standards and any processes mandatedby the Information Security Management System (ISMS).

3.5.2 ISO/IEC 17799:

BS 7799 / ISO 17799 meet the needs of organizations and companies of all types, both private and public. For any organization that stores confidential information on internal or external systems, depends on such systems to run its operations, or indeed wishes to demonstrate its information security by conforming to a known standard, BS 7799 / ISO 17799 would be of very great interest. The following chart illustrates the many possible uses of the standard.

Type of company	Size	Primary objective	Use of the standard
Small enterprise or organization	Less than 200 employees	Raise management's awareness regarding information security	ISO 17799 contains the security topics that should be dealt with as a foundation for management.
Medium enterprise (centralized or decentralized)	Less than 5000 employees	Create a compatible corporate security culture	The standard contains the practices required to put together an information security policy.
Large enterprise	More than 5000 employees	Obtain security certification at the end of the process	Use BS 7799-2 to create an internal security reference document.

Benefits of the ISO 17799 standard

ISO 17799 standard certification does not in itself prove that an organization is 100% secure. The truth is, barring acessation of all activity, there is no such thing as complete security. Nevertheless, adopting this international standard conferscertain advantages that any manager should take into consideration, including:

Organizational level- Commitment: certification serves as a promise of the effectiveness of the effort put into rendering the enterprise secure at all levels, and demonstrates the due caution of its administrators.

Legal level- Compliance: certification demonstrates to competent authorities that the organization observes all applicable laws and regulations. In this matter, the standard complements other existing standards and legislation.

Operating level-Risk management: leads to a better knowledge of information systems, their weaknesses and how to protect them. Equally, it ensures a more dependable availability of both hardware and data.

Commercial level-Credibility and confidence: partners, shareholders and customers are reassured when they see the importance afforded by the organization to protecting information. Certification can help set a company apart from its competitors and in the market place. Already, international invitations to tender are starting to require ISO 17799 compliance.

Financial level- Reduced costs related to security breaches and possible reduction in insurance premiums.

Human level-Improves employee awareness of security issues and their responsibilities within the organization. While ISO 17799 sets out the best practices for managing information security and creating security policies, ISO 13335, also called GMITS - Guidelines for the Management of IT Security - is its big brother. This standard deals more with the technological aspects of information, and brings value-added content to risk assessment. The protective measures proposed in the fourth of ISO 13335's five guides could be compared to the controls offered in ISO 17799.There is also a strong complementarity between ISO 17799 and ISO 15408. The latter, better known under the name Common Criteria, certifies the levels of defense conferred by the security measures in information systems. It therefore covers technical aspects, here as ISO 17799 focuses more on the organizational and administrative aspects of security.

3.5.3 ISO 27001:

ISO27001 was developed by the International Organization for Standardization (ISO) and the International Electro technical Commission (IEC) as a certification standard for information security management systems. ISO27001 certification can be a powerful credential for an organization, showing that their IT security policy follows an international standard of due care.

ISO27001 is designed to be used in conjunction with the ISO 17799:2005. Best practice recommendations for information security management. To achieve ISO27001 certification, organizations much adopt a risk-based approach that uses the security controls specified within ISO 17799:2005.

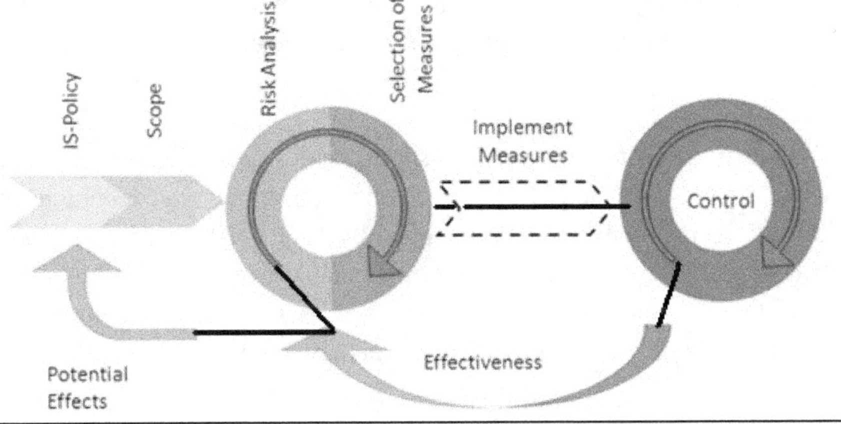

Information Shield has the tools your organization needs to save money while developing an IT security policy that will enable ISO27001 certification.

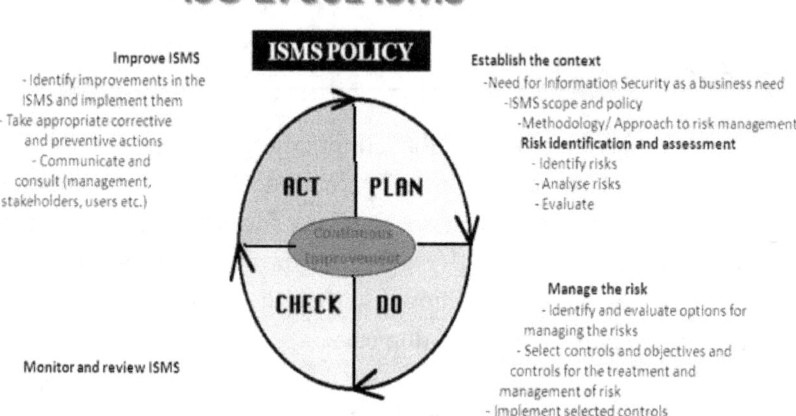

Information Security Policies Made Easy provides over 1300 security policies built within the ISO 17799:2005 framework. The ISO 17799:2005 policy map outlines the security policies that will lead you to ISO27001 certification, providing coverage of each security domain and sub-clause.

Information Security Roles and Responsibilities Made Easy is a perfect companion product, helping your organization define and document the roles and responsibilities recommended by ISO 17799:2005. It includes job descriptions with security requirements, organizational charts, and departmental mission statements all designed to facilitate your organization's move to compliance and certification.

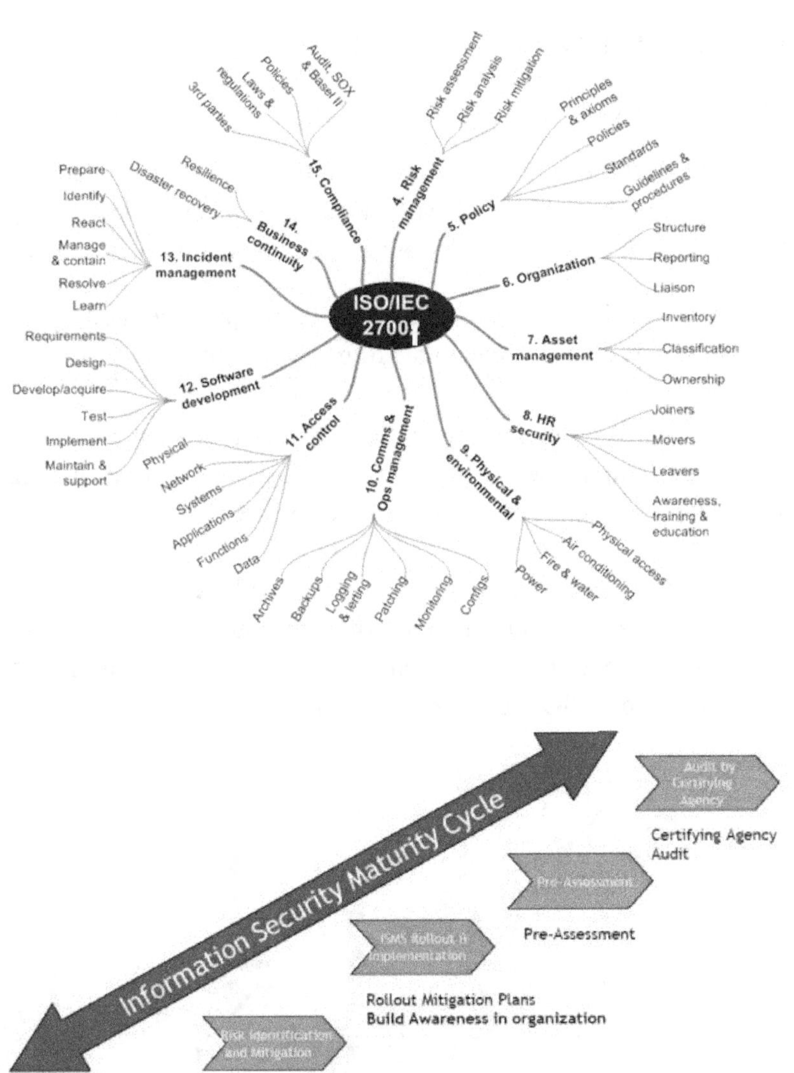
Audit, SOX & Basel II
Policies
Laws & regulations
3rd parties
Risk assessment
Risk analysis
Risk mitigation
Principles & axioms
Policies
Standards
Guidelines & procedures
15. Compliance
4. Risk management
5. Policy
ISO/IEC 27001
Resilience
Disaster recovery
14. Business continuity
6. Organization
Structure
Reporting
Liaison
Prepare
Identify
React
Manage & contain
Resolve
Learn
13. Incident management
7. Asset management
Inventory
Classification
Ownership
Requirements
Design
Develop/acquire
Test
Implement
Maintain & support
12. Software development
8. HR security
Joiners
Movers
Leavers
Awareness, training & education
Physical
Network
Systems
Applications
Functions
Data
11. Access control
10. Comms & Ops management
9. Physical & environmental
Physical access
Air conditioning
Fire & water
Power
Archives
Backups
Logging & lerting
Patching
Monitoring
Configs
Information Security Maturity Cycle
Audit by Certifying Agency
Certifying Agency Audit
Pre-Assessment
Pre-Assessment
ISMS Rollout & Implementation
Rollout Mitigation Plans
Build Awareness in organization
Risk Identification and Mitigation
Create Risk Treatment Plan
Design Information Security Policies
Define the Business Continuity Management Plan
Re-design Security Architecture
Definition of ISMS
Define Business Objectives
Conduct Information Risk Assessment
Create Statement of Applicability

3.5.4 ISO IES 27002 2005 IS Audit Tool:

This standard comes in two parts:

ISO/IEC 27001:2005 – is a standard specification for an Information Security Management Systems (ISMS) which instructs you how to apply ISO/IEC 27002 and how to build, operate, maintain and improve ISMS.

ISO/IEC 27002:2007 - is a standard code of practice and can be regarded as a comprehensive catalogue of good security things to do

---

Information Security Policies Made Easy does more than just enable development of your IT security policy. It shows you how to maintain and monitor those policies as required by the certification process.

Why re-invent the wheel? We can provide you with detailed IT security policy solutions, saving you hundreds of man-hours and thousands of dollars. Please contact Information Shield today for more information how we can help your ISO27001 certification.

- Gives recommendations for information security management for use by those who are responsible for initiating, implementing or maintaining security in their organization.

- It is intended to provide a common basis for developing organizational security standards and effective security management practice and to provide confidence in inter-organizational dealings.

Recommendations from this standard should be selected and used in accordance with applicable laws and regulations.

- Information security policy document

- Review and evaluation

- Information security is a business responsibility shared by all members of the management team."

- Information security infrastructure

- **Management Framework**: management for a with management leadership should be established to approve the information security policy, assign security roles and co-ordinate the implementation of security across the organization

- **Multi-Disciplinary:** approach to information security: involving the co-operation and collaboration of managers, users, administrators, application designers, auditors and security staff, and specialist skills in areas such as insurance and ``

a) ISO-27001 ISMS Tool Kit

The hardest part of achieving ISO27001 certification is providing the documentation of the Information Security Management System (ISMS). The documentation that is necessary to create a conforming system, particularly in more complex businesses.

Benefits of an ISO27001 Documentation Toolkit

A toolkit can accelerate your ISO27001 project immensely. The key benefits of using a documentation toolkit are:

- Provides clear guidance on the role of the risk assessment

- Template documents are easy to edit and customize

- Template documents save you time on research

- Template documents save you time on procedure writing

- This toolkit contains ten years of ISO27001 implementation experience - so you get tested, pragmatic solutions.

- It is precisely tailored to the requirements of ISO27001/ISO27002 – it doesn't contain hundreds and hundreds of generic policies (ISO27001 only requires seven), but it does contain exactly the documents that you will need if you are serious about achieving certification – so your customization time is minimized.

- It is comprehensive:

There are 6 versions of the ISO27001 Toolkit, all of which include the Standalone ISO27001 ISMS 27001 Documentation Toolkit. The Standalone Toolkit includes:

- A model Information Security Policy

- A model Statement of Applicability

- Pre-written Information Security Manual

- Risk assessment tool Integration Templates

- A Business Continuity Plan

- Gap analysis ISO27001: 2013 and ISO27002: 2013 Audit tool

- Gap analysis tool: ISO27001: 2005 to ISO27001: 2013

- New documentation developed for Asset Management, Supplier Relationships, Operations and Communications Security, etc.

3.6 Understanding Laws for Information Security:

To do this, security professionals must be knowledgeable on laws pertaining to privacy, civil and criminal activity. This encompasses understanding the issues of investigating computer crimes, the role of forensics, types of evidence and how to ensure that companies are compliant to applicable laws.

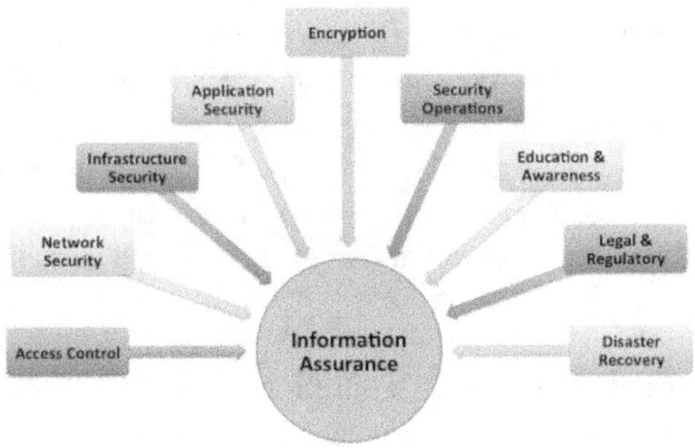

Above all, security professionals must be prepared to apply prudent judgment, often in tense situations, so that appropriate decisions will be made. This domain of the CISSP® Common Body of Knowledge covers the following topics:

- **Professional ethics:** Ethics as they pertain to security professionals and best practices

- **Cyber law and crimes:** Types of computer crimes, and the laws and acts put into effect to fight computer crime

- **Motives and profiles of attackers:** Attack profiles, types and objectives

- **Incident handling and investigation techniques:** Computer crime investigation procedures, including types of evidence and handling procedures

Professional ethics

Security professionals are expected to know and respect the laws and regulations governing the use of computers and information. Ethics are the rules that we fall back on when the letter of the law does not pertain to a particular situation or does not provide clear direction for a particular circumstance.

When becoming a CISSP, one must agree to accept and uphold the (ISC)2 Code of Professional Ethics, which set standards of behavior for security professionals. They range from commonsense guidance, such as "act honestly, justly, responsibly and protect society" to "stay current on skills..." These obligations are essential to building trust in the security profession that engenders respect from management and other professionals. Without this respect and trust, it is difficult to do the job to its full extent.

Several other organizations also offer ethical guidance and are covered in the law, investigation and ethics domain. These organizations include The Computer Ethics Institute, the Internet Architecture Board (IAB) and those of the Generally Accepted Information Security Principles (GAISP) Committee. They all provide similar expectations. As an information security professional, your behavior and actions are expected to be above reproach. Part of your responsibility is to demonstrate good information security behavior, to work to protect the privacy of others and to protect the assets of your organization. This domain also dispels some of the common ethical myths, such as "hacking is only illegal if you profit by it." Unauthorized hacking is a crime under most circumstances, and it is up to security professionals to help dispel such myths

What is information security?

Information security refers to the steps that we can take to:

- Ensure good data management.

- Protect information against damage, loss and theft.

- Protect the ICT equipment and systems used to collect, store and process that information.

Why is information security important?

Certain types of information are legally protected under the Data Protection Act (e.g. staff, student and medical records). Other types of information may be protected by a contractual agreement (e.g. financial or commercially sensitive data provided by a private sector company).

A failure to safeguard other people's personal information may cause them serious distress. In some cases, those people may become victims of crime. Negative publicity and regulatory action by the Information Commissioner's Office may also cause significant damage to the reputation of the University.

A failure to safeguard information that is protected by a contractual agreement may result in the University being refused access to important research funding and research data. Such an event may impact the University's ability to carry out research.

What are the threats?

The types of threat that may result in the damage, loss and theft of protected information include:

- Loss and theft of portable computing devices (e.g. laptops, tablet computers and smart phones) and portable storage devices (e.g. USB flash drives and external hard disk drives).

- The accidental publishing of confidential information on the Internet (e.g. social media, blogs and messaging boards).

- The sending of a confidential email to the wrong recipient.

- Large volumes of confidential printed information kept on desks.

- Confidential documents left on photocopiers and fax machines.

- Unlocked filing cabinets.

- Incorrect disposal of confidential information (e.g. failure to shred confidential paper waste, failure to securely erase computer data).

- Non-secure cloud computing (e.g. cloud service may be located in a country with no data protection laws).

- Scam emails sent by criminals in an attempt to obtain important personal information.

- Viruses and malicious software.

- Computer hackers.

Personal information is valued by criminals who will steal it for fraudulent purposes. In 2010 the National Fraud Authority revealed that

£1.9bn was fraudulently obtained in the UK through the theft of 1.8 million identities, averaging over £1000 for each victim.

PricewaterhouseCoopers revealed in their 2008 Information Security Breaches Survey that the loss and theft of portable computing devices and portable storage devices is a major cause of information security breaches in the work place.

3.7 Legislative Solutions:

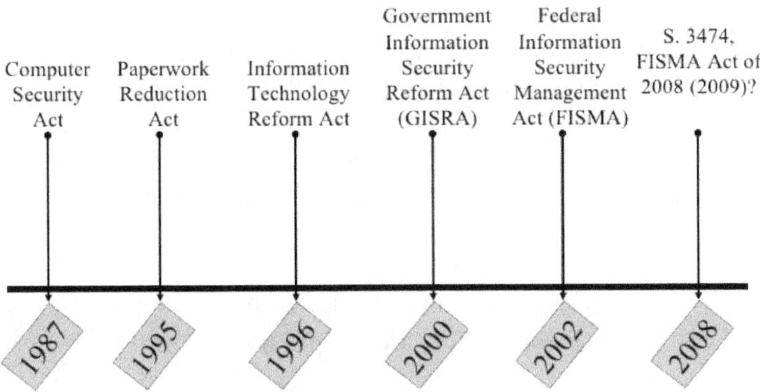

You need to be mindful of business associate agreement requirements and take the necessary steps to protect sensitive information and ensure your customers and businesses are in compliance. The following are questions you can ask yourself to help determine the impact compliance has on your business and whether you're taking the proper steps to minimize your own business risks:

1. What regulation – or set of regulations – is each of your customers responsible for? If you're not sure, just ask. If your customers aren't sure then perhaps you've got a new project in the works!

2. How is your business impacted by these regulations? Are you considered a business associate or an actual covered entity, which may be held to even higher standards?

3. What have you agreed to in customer contracts and customer policies? These agreements are often more stringent than industry regulations.

4. What sensitive information (i.e. credit card numbers, health care records and mortgage loan applications) do you collect, process, store or otherwise handle for customers? Don't overlook what's stored on unencrypted laptops, smart phones and backup tapes, as these tend to be areas a lot of people overlook and consequently get into trouble.

5. Are you really doing the best you can to protect sensitive customer (or third-party) information? Specifically:

   o Are all of your laptop hard drives and mobile storage devices used in the course of business encrypted with an enterprise full disk encryption solution?

   o Are your smart phones protected against loss, theft or malware?

   o Are you performing security assessments of your own environment (Web applications, databases, operating systems, network infrastructure devices, etc.) to find out where you're weak and how you can get hacked?

   o Do you have someone on staff who is in charge of monitoring industry and government regulations to ensure compliance and to seek out business opportunities?

Every situation is different. Every regulation is different. So is every business' risk tolerance. You'll even see a wide array of expectations from your customers when it comes to information security and compliance. Whatever you do, never fall into the mindset that compliance comes in a box. It doesn't.

It pays to be vigilant, and understand what you've signed up for and what security regulations your customers *and* your business are held to. Even if there are no laws, contracts or policies governing how you handle customer information (which is unlikely), it pays to do your own due diligence when protecting sensitive data by holding yourself to a high standard of information protection. You are the IT expert in the eyes of your customers. Not only is your guidance golden, you'll gain credibility and build trust by practicing what you preach.

Law firms continue to be a primary target for cyber criminals looking to gain access to intellectual property, trade secrets and other business capital. FBI officials have warned many times that law firms are a weak link and need to be more proactive to keep confidential information safe.

Managing the risks are not always easy. Imagine the paralegal who unknowingly clicks on a malicious link embedded with spyware; the junior lawyer who accidentally leaves his laptop in a taxi cap only to have it fall into the wrong hands; the managing partner who stores files on a cloud-based service, unaware of a possible entry point for a devastating breach.

At DDI we understand the risks and challenges that law firms face in today's market.

- It is crucial for a law firm to protect attorney client privileged information from access by unauthorized resources

- It's necessary to comply with information security regulations to guard personally identifiable information

- And it's common for law firms to have employees who are charged with defending data that are overwhelmed and unprepared

A **cyber security regulation** comprises directives that safeguard information technology and computer systems with the purpose of forcing companies and organizations to protect their systems and information from cyber-attacks. Cyber-attacks include viruses, worms, Trojan horses, phishing, denial of service (DOS) attacks, unauthorized access (stealing intellectual property or confidential information) and control system attacks. There are numerous measures available to prevent cyber-attacks. Cyber-security measures include firewalls, anti-virus software, intrusion detection and prevention systems, encryption and login passwords. There have been attempts to improve cyber security through regulation and collaborative efforts between government and the private-sector to encourage voluntary improvements to cyber security. Industry regulators including banking regulators have taken notice of the risk from cyber security and have either begun or are planning to begin to include cyber security as an aspect of regulatory examinations.

3.8 Contractual Solutions:

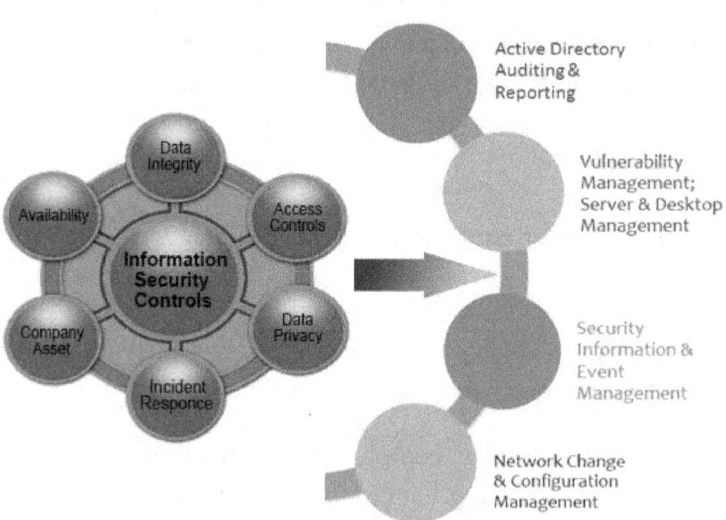

Contract Solutions-i is a multi-disciplinary dispute resolution practice founded by experienced construction, engineering and oil & gas industry practitioners. The firm comprises of engineers, quantity surveyors, construction managers, planners, accountants and other construction professionals, many of whom are dual qualified in law, adjudication and/or arbitration.

☐ An accurate, reliable, searchable, centralized contract management system.

☐ Collaborative creation and workflow of multi-lingual templates and contracts.

☐ Creation of a template repository with clause and library capabilities.

☐ Negotiation, escalation, and approval processes.

☐ Monitoring and alerting against milestones.

☐ Extensive reporting and analytical tools (e.g., audit tracking functionality).

☐ Roles, permissions, and security systems supporting multiple parties.

☐ Data import and export capabilities.

☐ Integration with other systems including web services API, CRM & ERP, and system integration (e.g., Salesforce, SAP, Oracle, Ariba, etc.).

☐ Sound security of data.

☐ Proven reliability, performance, and operational efficiency.

☐ Professional consulting, training, and support services.

☐ Paralegal and attorney support with contract review, template creation, redlining, negotiation, escalation, and approval capabilitie

3.9 Evidential Issues:

To the extent that the issue is one of evidence, California is governed by the limits of federal protection for the exclusionary rule. But to the extent that the issue is one of constitutional protection of privacy rights when private individuals are acting under color of law, decisions on how to define "color of law" may well be constitutional, not merely evidentiary. This is just a different way of defining that tennis volley to try to get the ball to land in the court you'd like it to be in, state or federal.

The evidentiary issue always comes up in connection with that of the exclusionary rule. Since the exclusionary rule is a judicial remedy, not a statute or a constitutional requirement, it requires the courts' application of precedent. And the courts are bound by the new constitutional amendment, art.1, sec. 28, subd.(d) which says that relevant evidence in a criminal proceeding shall not be excluded unless so required by the federal constitution.

The exclusionary rule is not a rule of evidence. It cannot be found in the evidence code. It is a judicial remedy which applies to the exclusion of evidence. Many courts have referred to the exclusionary rule as an evidentiary rule. But there is ample precedent for regarding the rule as one of constitutional law. That gives it greater weight than a mere rule of evidence.

Under the Code, the claimant – or the person making a claim – has the onus of proving an allegation of sexual harassment. A claimant must show a human rights tribunal that, on a "balance of probabilities," there appears to be a contravention of the Code. The burden of proof for showing harassment under the Code is not as strong as the "beyond a reasonable doubt" standard required for establishing guilt in criminal cases.

Proving a case on a "balance of probabilities" is a civil burden of proof, meaning that there is evidence to support the allegation that the comments or conduct "more likely than not" took place, and that the behavior was sexual harassment within the meaning of the Code.

Sexual harassment does not often occur in full public view. Since there are often no witnesses or material evidence to these comments or conduct, issues of credibility often arise in sexual harassment claims. Human rights tribunals have accepted that it is difficult sometimes to make a finding based on credibility only, but acknowledge that tribunals often have to rely on subjective evidence presented by the parties involved.

Repeated conduct directed at one person is not needed. A pattern of conduct directed at several female employees may also be sexual harassment. Where credibility is at issue, similar fact evidence may be introduced to show that a pattern of behavior might have occurred. Similar fact evidence could include testimony from others who state that they have been treated in the same way by the alleged harasser.

Example: A tribunal found that an employer misused "his business and his position of power within it to sexually solicit, harass and intimidate young women on job interviews and in their employment relationship with him." The tribunal found this behavior was "a highly distinctive pattern, or "signature" of discriminatory conduct toward young women who responded to job advertisements at his place of business." On this basis, the tribunal allowed evidence of multiple claimants to be entered as similar fact evidence.

Previous allegations or complaints of sexual harassment against an individual may be evidence that the person should reasonably have known that similar behavior in the future is not welcome.

As mentioned earlier, human rights law has established that the intention of the harasser does not matter when deciding if sexual harassment has occurred. The Supreme Court of Canada has held that a lack of intention is no defence to an allegation of discrimination. It is enough if the conduct has a discriminatory effect, and the focus should be on the impact of the questionable behaviour.

Example: A manager's special attention to a new female employee starts out as mentorship. However, his behaviour soon takes on overly personal overtones that include questions about her relationship with her boyfriend and her sexual past. The employee becomes more and more uncomfortable and tries to avoid being alone with her manager. Eventually, unsure of what else to do, she quits her job.

Note that a person does not have to object to the harassment at the time it happens for there to be a violation, or for the person to claim their rights under the Code.[A person who is the target of harassment may be in a vulnerable situation and afraid to speak out. Employers, housing providers, educators and other responsible parties must maintain an environment that is free of discrimination and harassment, whether or not anyone objects.

Courts and tribunals have also recognized that, due to the power imbalance that often exists between the harasser and the person being harassed, and the perceived consequences of objecting to the harassing behaviour, the person may go along with the unwelcome conduct.In The Law of Human Rights in Canada: Practice and Procedure, Russel Zinn notes:

The complainant's apparent passivity or failure to object overtly to sexual advances does not necessarily signal consent or welcomeness. This is particularly prevalent where there is an imbalance of power between the parties, such that the victim's dependence on the harasser's goodwill makes her more apt to tolerate unacceptable behaviour.

Even though a person being harassed may take part in sexual activity or other related behaviour, this does not mean they welcome it. Courts and tribunals have found that a power imbalance in a relationship can negate consent to sexual activity. This approach is consistent with the approach in other jurisdictions.

Where a person in a position of power is intent on pursuing an intimate relationship with an employee, tenant, student, etc., they are expected to go to great lengths to make sure the behaviour is welcome. Where a person is particularly vulnerable (for example, they are young, a probationary or temporary employee, etc.), the responsibility of the person in a position of power is even greater.

Past consent to sexual activity does not equal present consent when it is made clear that one party does not welcome further sexual interaction.

Human rights case law has found that depending on the circumstances, negative behaviour, including poor performance, outbursts, insubordination, etc. may be an understandable reaction to discrimination or harassment.

Example: After enduring months of unwanted attention from her professor, including numerous requests for dates, a university student begins to skip her classes, and ultimately fails her final examination.

Before taking punitive measures after such reactions, employers, housing providers, educators and other responsible parties should consider, where appropriate, whether the behaviour is in response to sexual harassment and should adjust their sanctions accordingly.

3.10 International Activity Indian IT Act:

Objectives of IT legislation in India:

The Government of India enacted its Information Technology Act 2000 with the objectives stating officially as:

"to provide legal recognition for transactions carried out by means of electronic data interchange and other means of electronic communication, commonly referred to as **"electronic commerce"**, which involve the use of alternatives to paper-based methods of communication and storage of information, to facilitate electronic filing of documents with the Government agencies and further to amend the Indian Penal Code, the Indian Evidence Act, 1872, the Bankers' Books Evidence Act, 1891 and the Reserve Bank of India Act, 1934 and for matters connected therewith or incidental thereto."

What does IT Act 2000 legislation deals with?

The Act essentially deals with the following issues:

- Legal Recognition of Electronic Documents

- Legal Recognition of Digital Signatures

- Offenses and Contraventions

- Justice Dispensation Systems for cyber crimes.

Why did the need for IT Amendment Act 2008 (ITAA) arise?

The IT Act 2000, being the first legislation on technology, computers, e-commerce and e-communication, the was the subject of extensive debates, elaborate reviews with one arm of the industry criticizing some sections of the Act to be draconian and other stating it is too diluted and lenient. There were some obvious omissions too resulting in the investigators relying more and more on the time-tested (one and half century-old) Indian Penal Code even in technology based cases with the IT Act also being referred in the process with the reliance more on IPC rather on the ITA.

Thus the need for an amendment – a detailed one – was felt for the I.T. Act. Major industry bodies were consulted and advisory groups were formed to go into the perceived lacunae in the I.T. Act and comparing it with similar legislations in other nations and to suggest recommendations. Such recommendations were analyzed and subsequently taken up as a comprehensive Amendment Act and after considerable administrative procedures; the consolidated amendment called the **Information Technology Amendment Act 2008** was placed in the Parliament and passed at the end of 2008 (just after Mumbai terrorist attack of 26 November 2008 had taken place). The IT Amendment Act 2008 got the President assent on 5 Feb 2009 and was made effective from 27 October 2009.

1. **Notable features of the ITAA 2008 are:**

- Focusing on data privacy

- Focusing on Information Security

- Defining cyber café

- Making digital signature technology neutral

- Defining reasonable security practices to be followed by corporate

- Redefining the role of intermediaries

- Recognizing the role of Indian Computer Emergency Response Team

- Inclusion of some additional cyber crimes like child pornography and cyber terrorism

- Authorizing an Inspector to investigate cyber offenses (as against the DSP earlier)

2. Structure of IT Act

- **How is IT Act structured?**

  The Act totally has 13 chapters and 90 sections. Sections 91 to 94 deal with the amendments to the four Acts namely Indian Penal Code 1860, The Indian Evidence Act 1872, The Bankers' Books Evidence Act 1891 and the Reserve Bank of India Act 1934. The Act has chapters that deal with authentication of electronic records, electronic signatures etc.

  Elaborate procedures for certifying authorities and electronic signatures have been spelt out. The civil offence of data theft and the process of adjudication and appellate procedures have been described. Then the Act goes on to define and describe some of the well-known cyber crimes and lays down the punishments therefore. Then the concept of due diligence, role of intermediaries and some miscellaneous provisions have been described.

- **What is the applicability of IT Act?**

The Act extends to the whole of India and except as otherwise provided, it also applies to any offence or contravention there under committed outside India by any person. Rules and procedures mentioned in the Act have also been laid down in a phased manner, defined as recently as April 2011. For the sake of simplicity, here we will be only discussing the various penalty and offences defined as per provisions of ITA 2000 and ITAA 2008. Please note that wherever the terms IT Act 2000 or 2008 are used, they refer to same act because the IT Act now includes amendments as per IT 2008 Amendment Act. Specific exclusion(s) to the Act where it is not applicable are:

o   Negotiable instrument (other than a cheque) as defined in section 13 of the Negotiable Instruments Act, 1881;

o   A power-of-attorney as defined in section 1A of the Powers-of-Attorney Act, 1882;

o   A trust as defined in section 3 of the Indian Trusts Act, 1882

o   A will as defined in clause (h) of section 2 of the Indian Succession Act, 1925 including any other testamentary disposition

3.   What is a cyber crime?

Cyber Crime is not defined officially in IT Act or in any other legislation. In fact, it cannot be too. Offence or crime has been dealt with elaborately listing various acts and the punishments for each, under the Indian Penal Code, 1860 and related legislations. Hence, the concept of cyber crime is just a "combination of crime and computer".

Cybercrime in a narrow sense (computer crime): Any illegal behavior directed by means of electronic operations that targets the security of computer systems and the data processed by them.

Cybercrime in a broader sense (computer-related crime): Any illegal behavior committed by means of, or in relation to, a computer system or network, including such crimes as illegal possession and offering or distributing information by means of a computer system or network.

*   Any contract for the sale or conveyance of immovable property or any interest in such property;

- Any such class of documents or transactions as may be notified by the Central Government

4. Cases Studies as per selected IT Act Sections

Here are the case studies for selected IT Act sections.

For the sake of simplicity and maintaining clarity, details on the IT Act sections have been omitted. Kindly refer the Appendix at the last section for the detailed account of all the penalties and offences mentioned in IT Act.

- **Section 43 – Penalty and Compensation for damage to computer, computer system, etc Related Case: Mphasis BPO Fraud: 2005** In December 2004, four call centre employees, working at an outsourcing facility operated by MphasiS in India, obtained PIN codes from four customers of MphasiS' client, Citi Group. These employees were not authorized to obtain the PINs. In association with others, the call centre employees opened new accounts at Indian banks using false identities. Within two months, they used the PINs and account information gleaned during their employment at MphasiS to transfer money from the bank accounts of CitiGroup customers to the new accounts at Indian banks. By April 2005, the Indian police had tipped off to the scam by a U.S. bank, and quickly identified the individuals involved in the scam. Arrests were made when those individuals attempted to withdraw cash from the falsified accounts, $426,000 was stolen; the amount recovered was $230,000. **Verdict**: Court held that Section 43(a) was applicable here due to the nature of unauthorized access involved to commit transactions.

- **Section 65 – Tampering with Computer Source Documents**

Related Case: Syed Asifuddin and Ors. Vs. The State of Andhra Pradesh In this case, Tata Indicom employees were arrested for manipulation of the electronic 32- bit number (ESN) programmed into cell phones theft were exclusively franchised to Reliance Infocomm.

Verdict: Court held that tampering with source code invokes Section 65 of the Information Technology Act.

- **Section 66 – Computer Related offenses Related Case: Kumar v/s Whiteley** In this case the accused gained unauthorized access to the Joint Academic Network (JANET) and deleted, added files and changed the passwords to deny access to the authorized users.Investigations had revealed that Kumar was logging on to the BSNL broadband Internet connection as if he was the authorized genuine user and 'made alteration in the computer database pertaining to broadband Internet user accounts' of the subscribers.The CBI had registered a cyber crime case against Kumar and carried out investigations on the basis of a complaint by the Press Information Bureau, Chennai, which detected the unauthorised use of broadband Internet. The complaint also stated that the subscribers had incurred a loss of Rs 38,248 due to Kumar's wrongful act. He used to 'hack' sites from Bangalore, Chennai and other cities too, they said.

Verdict: The Additional Chief Metropolitan Magistrate, Egmore, Chennai, sentenced N G Arun Kumar, the techie from Bangalore to undergo a rigorous imprisonment for one year with a fine of Rs 5,000 under section 420 IPC (cheating) and Section 66 of IT Act (Computer related Offense).

- **Section 66A – Punishment for sending offensive messages through communication service**

- **Relevant Case #1: Fake profile of President posted by imposter** On September 9, 2010, the imposter made a fake profile in the name of the Hon'ble President Pratibha Devi Patil. A complaint was made from Additional Controller, President Household, President Secretariat regarding the four fake profiles created in the name of Hon'ble President on social networking website, Facebook.The said complaint stated that president house has nothing to do with the facebook and the fake profile is misleading the general public. The First Information Report Under Sections 469 IPC and 66A Information Technology Act, 2000 was registered based on the said complaint at the police station, Economic Offences Wing, the elite wing of Delhi Police which specializes in investigating economic crimes including cyber offences.

- **Relevant Case #2: Bomb Hoax mail** In 2009, a 15-year-old Bangalore teenager was arrested by the cyber crime investigation cell (CCIC) of the city crime branch for allegedly sending a hoax e-mail to a private news channel. In the e-mail, he claimed to have planted five bombs in Mumbai, challenging the police to find them before it was too late. At around 1p.m. on May 25, the news channel received an e-mail that read: "I have planted five bombs in Mumbai; you have two hours to find it." The police, who were alerted immediately, traced the Internet Protocol (IP) address to Vijay Nagar in Bangalore. The Internet service provider for the account was BSNL, said officials.

- **Section 66C – Punishment for identity theft**

Relevant Cases:

- The CEO of an identity theft protection company, Lifelock, Todd Davis's social security number was exposed by Matt Lauer on NBC's Today Show. Davis' identity was used to obtain a $500 cash advance loan.

- Li Ming, a graduate student at West Chester University of Pennsylvania faked his own death, complete with a forged obituary in his local paper. Nine months later, Li attempted to obtain a new driver's license with the intention of applying for new credit cards eventually.

- **Section 66D – Punishment for cheating by impersonation by using computer resource Relevant Case: Sandeep Vaghese v/s State of Kerala**

A complaint filed by the representative of a Company, which was engaged in the business of trading and distribution of petrochemicals in India and overseas, a crime was registered against nine persons, alleging offenses under Sections 65, 66, 66A, C and D of the Information Technology Act along with Sections 419 and 420 of the Indian Penal Code.

The company has a web-site in the name and style 'www.jaypolychem.com' but, another web site 'www.jayplychem.org' was set up in the internet by first accused Samdeep Varghese @ Sam, (who was dismissed from the company) in conspiracy with other accused, including Preeti and Charanjeet Singh, who are the sister and brother-in-law of 'Sam'

Defamatory and malicious matters about the company and its directors were made available in that website. The accused sister and brother-in-law were based in

Cochin and they had been acting in collusion known and unknown persons, who have collectively cheated the company and committed acts of forgery, impersonation etc.

Two of the accused, Amardeep Singh and Rahul had visited Delhi and Cochin. The first accused and others sent e-mails from fake e-mail accounts of many of the customers, suppliers, Bank etc. to malign the name and image of the Company and its Directors. The defamation campaign run by all the said persons named above has caused immense damage to the name and reputation of the   Company.
The Company suffered losses of several crores of Rupees from producers, suppliers and customers and were unable to do business.

- **Section 66E – Punishment for violation of privacy**

Relevant Cases:

i.   **Jawaharlal Nehru University MMS scandal** In a severe shock to the prestigious and renowned institute – Jawaharlal Nehru University, a pornographic MMS clip was apparently made in the campus and transmitted outside the university.Some media reports claimed that the two accused students initially tried to extort money from the girl in the video but when they failed the culprits put the video out on mobile phones, on the internet and even sold it as a CD in the blue film market.

ii.   **Nagpur Congress leader's son MMS scandal** On January 05, 2012 Nagpur Police arrested two engineering students, one of them a son of a Congress leader, for harassing a 16-year-old girl by circulating an MMS clip of their sexual acts. According to the Nagpur (rural) police, the girl was in a relationship with Mithilesh Gajbhiye, 19, son of Yashodha Dhanraj Gajbhiye, a zila parishad member and an influential Congress leader of Saoner region in Nagpur district.

Section-66F Cyber Terrorism

Relevant Case: The Mumbai police have registered a case of 'cyber terrorism'—the first in the state since an amendment to the Information Technology Act—where a threat email was sent to the BSE and NSE on Monday. The MRA Marg police and the Cyber Crime Investigation Cell are jointly probing the case. The suspect has been detained in this case.The police said an email challenging the security agencies to prevent a terror attack was sent by one Shahab Md with an ID sh.itaiyeb125@yahoo.in to BSE's administrative email ID corp.relations@bseindia.com at around 10.44 am on Monday.The IP address of the sender has been traced to Patna in Bihar. The ISP is Sify. The email ID was created just four minutes before the email was sent. "The sender had, while creating the new ID, given two mobile numbers in the personal details column. Both the numbers belong to a photo frame-maker in Patna,'' said an officer.

Status: The MRA Marg police have registered forgery for purpose of cheating, criminal intimidation cases under the IPC and a cyber-terrorism case under the IT Act.

Section 67 – Punishment for publishing or transmitting obscene material in electronic form

Relevant Case: This case is about posting obscene, defamatory and annoying message about a divorcee woman in the Yahoo message group. E-mails were forwarded to the victim for information by the accused through a false e- mail account opened by him in the name of the victim. These postings resulted in annoying phone calls to the lady. Based on the lady's complaint, the police nabbed the accused.Investigation revealed that he was a known family friend of the victim and was interested in marrying her. She was married to another person, but that marriage ended in divorce and the accused started contacting her once again. On her reluctance to marry him he started harassing her through internet.

Verdict: The accused was found guilty of offences under section 469, 509 IPC and 67 of IT Act 2000. He is convicted and sentenced for the offence as follows:

- As per 469 of IPC he has to undergo rigorous imprisonment for 2 years and to pay fine of Rs.500/-

- As per 509 of IPC he is to undergo to undergo 1 year Simple imprisonment and to pay Rs 500/-

- As per Section 67 of IT Act 2000, he has to undergo for 2 years and to pay fine of Rs.4000/-

All sentences were to run concurrently.

The accused paid fine amount and he was lodged at Central Prison, Chennai. This is considered the first case convicted under section 67 of Information Technology Act 2000 in India.

Section 67B – Punishment for publishing or transmitting of material depicting children in sexually explicit act, etc. in electronic form

Relevant Case: Janhit Manch & Ors. v. The Union of India 10.03.2010 Public Interest Litigation: The petition sought a blanket ban on pornographic websites. The NGO had argued that websites displaying sexually explicit content had an adverse influence, leading youth on a delinquent path.

Section 69 – Powers to issue directions for interception or monitoring or decryption of any information through any computer resource

Relevant Case: In August 2007, Lakshmana Kailash K., a techie from Bangalore was arrested on the suspicion of having posted insulting images of Chhatrapati Shivaji, a major historical figure in the state of Maharashtra, on the social-networking site Orkut.The police identified him based on IP address details obtained from Google and Airtel - Lakshmana's ISP. He was brought to Pune and detained for 50 days before it was discovered that the IP address provided by Airtel was erroneous. The mistake was evidently due to the fact that while requesting information from Airtel, the police had not properly specified whether the suspect had posted the content at 1:15 p.m. **Verdict:** Taking cognizance of his plight from newspaper accounts, the State Human Rights Commission subsequently ordered the company to pay Rs 2 lakh to Lakshmana as damages. The incident highlights how minor privacy violations by ISPs and intermediaries could have impacts that gravely undermine other basic human rights.

5. Common Cyber-crime scenarios and Applicability of Legal Sections

Let us look into some common cyber-crime scenarios which can attract prosecution as per the penalties and offences prescribed in IT Act 2000 (amended via 2008) Act.

- **Harassment via fake public profile on social networking site**

  A fake profile of a person is created on a social networking site with the correct address, residential information or contact details but he/she is labelled as 'prostitute' or a person of 'loose character'. This leads to harassment of the victim.Provisions Applicable:- Sections 66A, 67 of IT Act and Section 509 of the Indian Penal Code.

- **Online Hate Community**

  Online hate community is created inciting a religious group to act or pass objectionable remarks against a country, national figures etc.Provisions Applicable:

Section 66A of IT Act and 153A & 153B of the Indian Penal Code.

- **Email Account Hacking**

  If victim's email account is hacked and obscene emails are sent to people in victim's address book.Provisions Applicable:- Sections 43, 66, 66A, 66C, 67, 67A and 67B of IT Act.

- **Credit Card Fraud**

  Unsuspecting victims would use infected computers to make online transactions.Provisions Applicable:- Sections 43, 66, 66C, 66D of IT Act and section 420 of the IPC.

- **Web Defacement**

  The homepage of a website is replaced with a pornographic or defamatory page. Government sites generally face the wrath of hackers on symbolic days.Provisions Applicable:- Sections 43 and 66 of IT Act and Sections 66F, 67 and 70 of IT Act also apply in some cases.

- **Introducing Viruses, Worms, Backdoors, Rootkits, Trojans, Bugs**

  All of the above are some sort of malicious programs which are used to destroy or gain access to some electronic information.Provisions Applicable:- Sections 43, 66, 66A of IT Act and Section 426 of Indian Penal Code.

- **Cyber Terrorism**

  Many terrorists are use virtual (GDrive, FTP sites) and physical storage media(USB's, hard drives) for hiding information and records of their illicit business.Provisions Applicable: Conventional terrorism laws may apply along with Section 69 of IT Act.

- **Online sale of illegal Articles**

  Where sale of narcotics, drugs weapons and wildlife is facilitated by the InternetProvisions Applicable:- Generally conventional laws apply in these cases.

- **Cyber Pornography**

  Among the largest businesses on Internet Pornography may not be illegal in many countries, but child pornography is Provisions Applicable:- Sections 67, 67A and 67B of the IT Act.

- **Phishing and Email Scams**

  Phishing involves fraudulently acquiring sensitive information through masquerading a site as a trusted entity.(E.g.Passwords,credit card information)Provisions Applicable:- **Section 66, 66A and 66D of IT Act and Section 420 of IPC**

- **Theft of Confidential Information**

  Many business organizations store their confidential information in computer systems. This information is targeted by rivals, criminals and disgruntled employees.Provisions Applicable:- Sections 43, 66, 66B of IT Act and Section 426 of Indian Penal Code.

- **Source Code Theft**

  A Source code generally is the most coveted and important "crown jewel" asset of a company.Provisions applicable:- Sections 43, 66, 66B of IT Act and Section 63 of Copyright Act.

- **Tax Evasion and Money Laundering**

  Money launderers and people doing illegal business activities hide their information in virtual as well as physical activities.Provisions Applicable: Income Tax Act and Prevention of Money Laundering Act. IT Act may apply case-wise.

- **Online Share Trading Fraud**

  It has become mandatory for investors to have their demat accounts linked with their online banking accounts which are generally accessed unauthorized, thereby leading to share trading frauds.Provisions Applicable: Sections 43, 66, 66C, 66D of IT Act and Section 420 of IPC

6. **Appendix**

    I. **Penalties, Compensation and Adjudication sections**

        - **Section 43 – Penalty and Compensation for damage to computer, computer system**
          If any person without permission of the owner or any other person who is in-

charge of a computer, computer system or computer network –

- o Accesses or secures access to such computer, computer system or computer network or computer resource

- o Downloads, copies or extracts any data, computer data, computer database or information from such computer, computer system or computer network including information or data held or stored in any removable storage medium;

- o Introduces or causes to be introduced any computer contaminant or computer virus into any computer, computer system or computer network-

- o Damages or causes to be damaged any computer, computer system or computer network, data, computer database, or any other programmes residing in such computer, computer system or computer network-

- o Disrupts or causes disruption of any computer, computer system, or computer network;

- o Denies or causes the denial of access to any person authorised to access any computer, computer system or computer network by any means

- o Charges the services availed of by a person to the account of another person by tampering with or manipulating any computer of a computer, computer system or computer network-

- o Provides any assistance to any person to facilitate access to a computer, computer system or computer network in contravention of the provisions of this Act, rules or regulations made there under,

- o Charges the services availed of by a person to the account of another person by tampering with or manipulating any computer, computer system, or computer network,

- o Destroys, deletes or alters any information residing in a computer resource or diminishes its value or utility or affects it injuriously by any means,

- o Steals, conceals, destroys or alters or causes any person to steal, conceal, destroy or alter any computer source code used for a computer resource with an intention to cause damage, he shall be liable to pay damages by way of compensation to the person so affected.

- **Section 43A – Compensation for failure to protect data** Where a body corporate, possessing, dealing or handling any sensitive personal data or information in a computer resource which it owns, controls or operates, is negligent in implementing and maintaining reasonable security practices and procedures and thereby causes wrongful loss or wrongful gain to any person, such body corporate shall be liable to pay damages by way of compensation, not exceeding five crore rupees, to the person so affected.

- **Section 44 – Penalty for failure to furnish information or return, etc.** If any person who is required under this Act or any rules or regulations made there under to –

  - Furnish any document, return or report to the Controller or the Certifying Authority, fails to furnish the same, he shall be liable to a penalty not exceeding one lakh and fifty thousand rupees for each such failure;

  - File any return or furnish any information, books or other documents within the time specified therefore in the regulations, fails to file return or furnish the same within the time specified therefore in the regulations, he shall be liable to a penalty not exceeding five thousand rupees for every day during which such failure continues:

o Maintain books of account or records, fails to maintain the same, he shall be liable to a penalty not exceeding ten thousand rupees for every day during which the failure continues.

- **Section 45 – Residuary Penalty** Whoever contravenes any rules or regulations made under this Act, for the contravention of which no penalty has been separately provided, shall be liable to pay a compensation not exceeding twenty-five thousand rupees to the person affected by such contravention or a penalty not exceeding twenty-five thousand rupees.

- **Section 47 – Factors to be taken into account by the adjudicating officer** Section 47 lays down that while adjudging the quantum of compensation under this Act, an adjudicating officer shall have due regard to the following factors, namely :-

- o The amount of gain of unfair advantage, wherever quantifiable, made as a result of the default;

- o The amount of loss caused to the person as a result of the default,

- o The repetitive nature of the default.

Offences sections

Section 65 – Tampering with Computer Source Documents If any person knowingly or intentionally conceals, destroys code or alters or causes another to conceal, destroy code or alter any computer, computer program, computer system, or computer network, he shall be punishable with imprisonment up to three years, or with fine up to two lakh rupees, or with both.

Section 66– Computer Related Offences If any person, dishonestly, or fraudulently, does any act referred to in section 43,he shall be punishable with imprisonment for a term which may extend to two three years or with fine which may extend to five lakh rupees or with both.

Section 66A – Punishment for sending offensive messages through communication service

Any person who sends, by means of a computer resource or a communication device,

- o Any information that is grossly offensive or has menacing character;

- o Any information which he knows to be false, but for the purpose of causing annoyance, inconvenience,danger,insult obstruction,injury,criminal intimidation, enmity, hatred, or ill will, persistently makes by making use of such computer resource or a communication device,

- o Any electronic mail or electronic mail message for the purpose of causing annoyance or inconvenience or to deceive or to mislead the addressee or recipient about the origin of such messages shall be punishable with imprisonment for a term which may extend to three years and with fine.

Section 66B – Punishment for dishonestly receiving stolen computer resource or communication device.

Whoever dishonestly receives or retains any stolen computer resource or communication device knowing or having reason to believe the same to be stolen computer resource or communication device, shall be punished with imprisonment of either description for a term which may extend to three years or with fine which may extend to rupees one lakh or with both.

Section 66C – Punishment for identity theft Whoever, fraudulently or dishonestly make use of the electronic signature, password or any other unique identification feature of any other person,shall be punished with imprisonment of either description for a term which may extend to three years and shall also be liable to fine which may extend to rupees one lakh.

Section 66D – Punishment for cheating by personation by using computer resource Whoever, by means of any communication device or computer resource cheats by personating; shall be punished with imprisonment of either description for a term which may extend to three years and shall also be liable to fine which may extend to one lakh rupees.

Section 66E – Punishment for violation of privacy Whoever, intentionally or knowingly captures, publishes or transmits the image of a private area of any person without his or her consent, under circumstances violating the privacy of that person, Explanation – For the purposes of this section:

    a. "transmit" means to electronically send a visual image with the intent that it be viewed by a person or persons;

    b. "capture", with respect to an image, means to videotape, photograph, film or record by any means;

    c. "private area" means the naked or undergarment clad genitals, pubic area, buttocks or female breast;

    d. "publishes" means reproduction in the printed or electronic form and making it available for public;

e. "under circumstances violating privacy" means circumstances in which a person can have a reasonable expectation that–

    i. he or she could disrobe in privacy, without being concerned that an image of his private area was being captured; or

    ii. any part of his or her private area would not be visible to the public, regardless of whether that person is in a public or private place.

shall be punished with imprisonment which may extend to three years or with fine not exceeding two lakh rupees, or with both.

Section-66F Cyber Terrorism

- Whoever,-

    a. with intent to threaten the unity, integrity, security or sovereignty of India or to strike terror in the people or any section of the people by –

    i. denying or cause the denial of access to any person authorized to access computer resource; or

    ii. attempting to penetrate or access a computer resource without authorization or exceeding authorized access; or

    iii. introducing or causing to introduce any Computer Contaminant and by means of such conduct causes or is likely to cause death or injuries to persons or damage to or destruction of property or disrupts or knowing that it is likely to cause damage or disruption of supplies or services essential to the life of the community or adversely affect the critical information infrastructure specified under section 70, or

    b. knowingly or intentionally penetrates or accesses a computer resource without authorization or exceeding authorized

> access, and by means of such conduct obtains access to information, data or computer database that is restricted for reasons of the security of the State or foreign relations; or any restricted information, data or computer database, with reasons to believe that such information, data or computer database so obtained may be used to cause or likely to cause injury to the interests of the sovereignty and integrity of India, the security of the State, friendly relations with foreign States, public order, decency or morality, or in relation to contempt of court, defamation or incitement to an offence, or to the advantage of any foreign nation, group of individuals or otherwise, commits the offence of cyber terrorism.

- o Whoever commits or conspires to commit cyber terrorism shall be punishable with imprisonment which may extend to imprisonment for life.

Section 67 – Punishment for publishing or transmitting obscene material in electronic form

Whoever publishes or transmits or causes to be published in the electronic form, any material which is lascivious or appeals to the prurient interest or if its effect is such as to tend to deprave and corrupt persons who are likely, having regard to all relevant circumstances, to read, see or hear the matter contained or embodied in it,shall be punished on first conviction with imprisonment of either description for a term which may extend to two three years and with fine which may extend to five lakh rupees andin the event of a second or subsequent conviction with imprisonment of either description for a term which may extend to five years and also with fine which may extend to ten lakh rupees.

Section 67A – Punishment for publishing or transmitting of material containing sexually explicit act, etc. in electronic form

Whoever publishes or transmits or causes to be published or transmitted in the electronic form any material which contains sexually explicit act or conductshall be punished on first conviction with imprisonment of either description for a term which may extend to five years and with fine which may extend to ten lakh rupees andin the event of second or subsequent conviction with imprisonment of either description for a term which may extend to seven years and also with fine which may extend to ten lakh rupees.

Section 67B. Punishment for publishing or transmitting of material depicting children in sexually explicit act, etc. in electronic form

Whoever:-

- o publishes or transmits or causes to be published or transmitted material in any electronic form which depicts children engaged in sexually explicit act or conduct or

- o creates text or digital images, collects, seeks, browses, downloads, advertises, promotes, exchanges or distributes material in any electronic form depicting children in obscene or indecent or sexually explicit manner or

- o cultivates, entices or induces children to online relationship with one or more children for and on sexually explicit act or in a manner that may offend a reasonable adult on the computer resource or

- o facilitates abusing children online or

o   records in any electronic form own abuse or that of others pertaining to sexually explicit act with children,

shall be punished on first conviction with imprisonment of either description for a term which may extend to five years and with a fine which may extend to ten lakh rupees
and in the event of second or subsequent conviction with imprisonment of either description for a term which may extend to seven years and also with fine which may extend to ten lakh rupees:

Provided that the provisions of section 67, section 67A and this section does not extend to any book, pamphlet, paper, writing, drawing, painting, representation or figure in electronic form

Section 69 – Powers to issue directions for interception or monitoring or decryption of any information through any computer resource.-

10.   Where the central Government or a State Government or any of its officer specially authorized by the Central Government or the State Government, as the case may be, in this behalf may, if is satisfied that it is necessary or expedient to do in the interest of the sovereignty or integrity of India, defence of India, security of the State, friendly relations with foreign States or public order or for preventing incitement to the commission of any cognizable offence relating to above or for investigation of any offence, it may, subject to the provisions of sub-section (2), for reasons to be recorded in writing, by order, direct any agency of the appropriate

Government to intercept, monitor or decrypt or cause to be intercepted or monitored or decrypted any information transmitted received or stored through any computer resource.

11. The Procedure and safeguards subject to which such interception or monitoring or decryption may be carried out, shall be such as may be prescribed.

12. The subscriber or intermediary or any person in charge of the computer resource shall, when called upon by any agency which has been directed under sub section (1), extend all facilities and technical assistance to –

- o provide access to or secure access to the computer resource generating, transmitting, receiving or storing such information; or

- o intercept or monitor or decrypt the information, as the case may be; or

- o provide information stored in computer resource.

13. The subscriber or intermediary or any person who fails to assist the agency referred to in sub-section (3) shall be punished with an imprisonment for a term which may extend to seven years and shall also be liable to fine.

Section 69A – Power to issue directions for blocking for public access of any information through any computer resource

14. Where the Central Government or any of its officer specially authorized by it in this behalf is

satisfied that it is necessary or expedient so to do in the interest of sovereignty and integrity of India, defense of India, security of the State, friendly relations with foreign states or public order or for preventing incitement to the commission of any cognizable offence relating to above, it may subject to the provisions of sub-sections (2) for reasons to be recorded in writing, by order direct any agency of the Government or intermediary to block access by the public or cause to be blocked for access by public any information generated, transmitted, received, stored or hosted in any computer resource.

15. The procedure and safeguards subject to which such blocking for access by the public may be carried out shall be such as may be prescribed.

16. The intermediary who fails to comply with the direction issued under sub-section (1) shall be punished with an imprisonment for a term which may extend to seven years and also be liable to fine.

Section 69B. Power to authorize to monitor and collect traffic data or information through any computer resource for Cyber Security

17. The Central Government may, to enhance Cyber Security and for identification, analysis and prevention of any intrusion or spread of computer contaminant in the country, by notification in the official Gazette, authorize any agency of the Government to monitor and collect traffic data or information generated, transmitted, received or stored in any computer resource.

18.   The Intermediary or any person in-charge of the Computer resource shall when called upon by the agency which has been authorized under sub-section (1), provide technical assistance and extend all facilities to such agency to enable online access or to secure and provide online access to the computer resource generating, transmitting, receiving or storing such traffic data or information.

19.   The procedure and safeguards for monitoring and collecting traffic data or information, shall be such as may be prescribed.

20.   Any intermediary who intentionally or knowingly contravenes the provisions of subsection (2) shall be punished with an imprisonment for a term which may extend to three years and shall also be liable to fine.

Section 71 – Penalty for misrepresentation

Whoever makes any misrepresentation to, or suppresses any material fact from, the Controller or the Certifying Authority for obtaining any license or Electronic Signature Certificate, as the case may be, shall be punished with imprisonment for a term which may extend to two years, or with fine which may extend to one lakh rupees, or with both.

Section 72 – Breach of confidentiality and privacy

Any person who, in pursuant of any of the powers conferred under this Act, rules or regulations made there under, has secured access to any electronic record, book, register, correspondence, information, document or other material without the consent of the person concerned discloses such electronic record, book, register, correspondence, information, document or other material to any other person shall be punished with imprisonment for a term which may extend to two years, or with fine which may extend to one lakh rupees, or with both.

Section 72A – Punishment for Disclosure of information in breach of lawful contract

Any person including an intermediary who, while providing services under the terms of lawful contract, has secured access to any material containing personal information about another person, with the intent to cause or knowing that he is likely to cause wrongful loss or wrongful gain discloses, without the consent of the person concerned, or in breach of a lawful contract, such material to any other person shall be punished with imprisonment for a term which may extend to three years, or with a fine which may extend to five lakh rupees, or with both.

73. Penalty for publishing electronic Signature Certificate false in certain particulars.

21. No person shall publish a Electronic Signature Certificate or otherwise make it available to any other person with the knowledge that

   a. the Certifying Authority listed in the certificate has not issued it; or

   b. the subscriber listed in the certificate has not accepted it; or

   c. the certificate has been revoked or suspended, unless such publication is for the purpose of verifying a digital signature created prior to such suspension or revocation

22. Any person who contravenes the provisions of sub-section (1) shall be punished with imprisonment for a term which may extend to

two years, or with fine which may extend to one lakh rupees, or with both.

Section 74 – Publication for fraudulent purpose:

Whoever knowingly creates publishes or otherwise makes available a Electronic Signature Certificate for any fraudulent or unlawful purpose shall be punished with imprisonment for a term which may extend to two years, or with fine which may extend to one lakh rupees, or with both.

Section 75 – Act to apply for offence or contraventions committed outside India

23. Subject to the provisions of sub-section (2), the provisions of this Act shall apply also to any offence or contravention committed outside India by any person irrespective of his nationality.

24. For the purposes of sub-section (1), this Act shall apply to an offence or contravention committed outside India by any person if the act or conduct constituting the offence or contravention involves a computer, computer system or computer network located in India.

Section 77A – Compounding of Offences.

25. A Court of competent jurisdiction may compound offences other than offences for which the punishment for life or imprisonment for a term exceeding three years has been provided under this Act.Provided further that the Court shall not compound any offence where such offence affects the socio-economic

conditions of the country or has been committed against a child below the age of 18 years or a woman.

26.   The person accused of an offence under this act may file an application for compounding in the court in which offence is pending for trial and the provisions of section 265 B and 265C of Code of Criminal Procedures, 1973 shall apply.

Section 77B – Offences with three years imprisonment to be cognizable

Not with standing anything contained in Criminal Procedure Code 1973, the offence punishable with imprisonment of three years and above shall be cognizable and the offence punishable with imprisonment of three years shall be bailable.

Section 78 – Power to investigate offences

Notwithstanding anything contained in the Code of Criminal Procedure, 1973, a police officer not below the rank of Inspector shall investigate any offence under this Act.

3.11 Laws of IPR Indian:

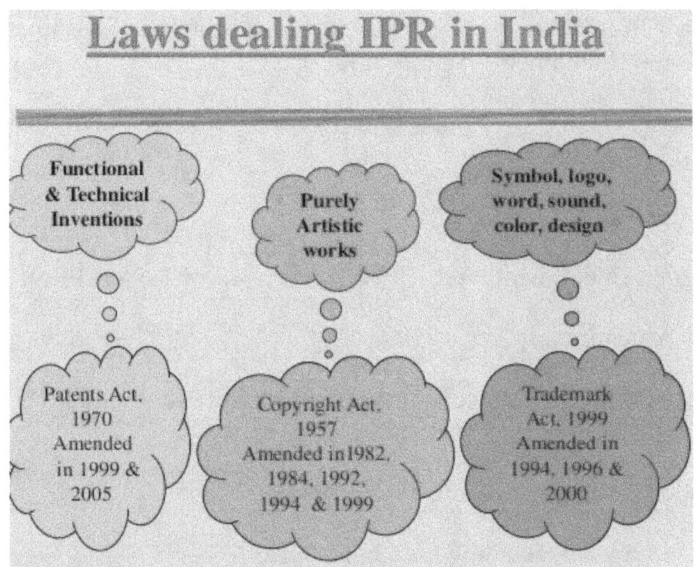

Main IP Laws: enacted by the Legislature

- The Semiconductor Integrated Circuits Layout-Designs Act, 2000 (Notification) (2014)

- The Copyright (Amendment) Act, 2012 (2012)

- The Trade Marks (Amendment) Act, 2010 (2010)

- The Competition (Amendment) Act, 2009 (2009)

- The Competition (Amendment) Act, 2007 (2007)

- Patents (Amendment) Act, 2005 (Act No. 15 of 2005) (2005)

- The Patents Act, 1970 (as amended up to Patents (Amendment) Act, 2005) (2005)

- The Semiconductor Integrated Circuits Layout-Design Act, 2000 (2004)

- The Geographical Indications of Goods (Registration and Protection) Act, 1999 (2003)

- The Trade Marks Act, 1999 (2003)

- Patents (Amendment) Act, 2002 (2002)

- Consumer Protection Act, 1986 (as amended up to the Consumer Protection (Amendment) Act, 2002) (2002)

- Protection of Plant Varieties and Farmers' Rights Act, 2001 (2001)

- The Designs Act, 2000 (2000)

- Copyright (Amendment) Act, 1999 (Act No. 49 of 1999) (1999)

- Patents (Amendment) Act, 1999 (1999)

- Copyright Act, 1957 (as consolidated up to Act No. 49 of 1999) (1999)

- Copyright (Amendment) Act, 1994 (1994)

  IP-related Laws: enacted by the Legislature

- The Customs Act, 1962

- The Companies Act, 2013 (No. 18 of 2013) (2015)

- The Prasar Bharati (Broadcasting Corporation of India) Amendment Act, 2011 (2012)

- The Cable Television Networks (Regulation) Amendment Act,2011 (2011)

- The Ancient Monuments and Archaeological Sites and Remains (Amendment and Validation) Act, 2010 (2010)

- The Prasar Bharati (Broadcasting Corporation of India) Amendment Act, 2008 (2008)

- The Cable Television Networks (Regulation) Amendment Act, 2007 (2007)

- The Micro, Small and Medium Enterprises Development Act, 2006 (2006)

- The Code of Criminal Procedure, 1973 (2006)

- The Competition Act 2002 (2003)

- Cable Television Networks (Regulation) Amendment Act, 2002 (2002)

- Biological Diversity Act, 2002 (2002)

- The Cable Television Networks (Regulation) Act, 1995 (2002)

- Cable Television Networks (Regulation) Amendment Act, 2000 (2000)

- The Information Technology Act, 2000 (2000)

- The Telecom Regulatory Authority of India (Amendment) Ordinance, 2000 (2000)

- The Prasar Bharati (Broadcasting Corporation of India) Act, 1990 (1997)

- The Arbitration And Conciliation Act, 1996 (1996)

- The Cinematograph Act, 1952 (1984)

- The Code of Civil Procedure, 1908 (1980)

- The Antiquities and Art Treasures Act, 1972 (1972)

- The Seeds (Amendment) Act, 1972 (1972)

- The Unlawful Activities (Prevention) Act, 1967 (Act No. 37 of 1967) (1967)

- The Seeds Act 1966 (1966)

- The Ancient Monuments and Archeological Sites and Remains Act, 1958 (1959)

- Indian Treasure Trove Act, 1878 (1949)

- The Indian Wireless Telegraph Act, 1933 (1933)

- The Indian Telegraph Act, 1885 (1885)

- Act No. IX of 1878 for better control of Publications in Oriental languages (1878)

- The Sea Customs Act, 1878 (1878)

- The Dramatic Performances Act, 1876 (1876)

- The Indian Penal Code (1860)

Implementing Rules/Regulations	Intellectual Property

- Patents (Amendment) Rules, 2016 (2016)

- Patents (Amendment) Rules, 2014 (2014)

- Radio Frequency devices or equipments including the Radio Frequency Identification Devices, (Exemption from Licensing Requirement) Rules, 2014 (2014)

- Gazette Notification of Trade Marks (Amendment) Rules, 2013 and Trade Marks (Amendment) Act, 2010 (2013)

- Patents (Amendment) Rules, 2013 (2013)

- Trade Marks (Amendment) Rules, 2013 (2013)

- The Copyright Rules, 2013 (2013)

- Patents Rules, 2003 (2013)

- Patents (Amendment) Rules, 2012 (2012)

- National Monuments Authority (Conditions of service of Chairman and Members of the Authority and Conduct of Business) Rules,2011 (2011)

- The Information Technology (Intermediaries guidelines) Rules, 2011 (2011)

- The Information Technology (Reasonable security practices and procedures and sensitive personal data or information) Rules, 2011 (2011)

- The Information Technology (Electronic Service Delivery) Rules, 2011 (2011)

- The Information Technology (Guidelines

for Cyber Cafe) Rules, 2011 (2011)

- Trade Marks (Amendment) Rules, 2010 (2010)

- Trade Marks (Second Amendment) Rules, 2010 (2010)

- Protection of Plant Varieties and Farmers Rights (Criteria for DUS for Registration) Regulations, 2009 (2009)

- Protection of Plant Varieties and Farmers' Rights (Third Amendment) Rules, 2009 (2009)

- Protection of Plant Varieties and Farmers' Rights (Second Amendment) Rules, 2009 (2009)

- The Cable Television Networks Rules, 1994 (as amended up to February 27, 2009) (2009)

- Direction of the Telecom Regulatory Authority of India (2008)

- Designs (Amendment) Rules, 2008 (2008)

- Circular on Implementing the Intellectual Property Rights (Imported Goods) Enforcement Rules, 2007 (2007)

- Intellectual Property Rights (Imported Goods) Enforcement Rules, 2007 (2007)

- Protection of Plant Varieties and Farmers' Rights Regulations, 2006 (2006)

- The Consumer Protection Rules, 1987 (as amended up to October 13, 2006) (2006)

- The National Board for Micro, Small and Medium Enterprises Rules, 2006 (2006)

- Patents (Amendment) Rules, 2006 (2006)

- Patents (Amendment) Rules, 2005 (2004)

- Biological Diversity Rules, 2004 (2004)

- The Drugs and Cosmetics Rules, 1945 (as corrected up to November 30, 2004) (2004)

- Protection of Plant Varieties and Farmer's Rights Rules, 2003 (2003)

- The Geographical Indications of Goods (Registration and Protection) Rules, 2002 (2002)

- Trade Marks Rules, 2002 (2002)

- Semiconductor Integrated Circuits Layout-Design Rules, 2001 (2001)

- The Designs Rules, 2001 (2001)

- Information Technology (Certifying Authorities) Rules, 2000 (2000)

- The International Copyright Order, 1999 (1999)

- The Telecom Regulatory Authority of India Act, 1997 (1997)

- The Antiquities and Art Treasure Rules 1973 (1973)

IP Legal Literature

- Classification Goods and Services (2013)

- Information Booklet for Applicants for Registration of Designs, © Office of the Controller General of Patents, Designs & Trade Marks (2010)

- Manual of Patent Office Practice and Procedure, 2010, © Office of the Controller General of Patents, Designs & Trade Marks

(2010)

- Intellectual Property Rights Policy for Kerala 2008, © Law Department, Government of Kerala (2008)

- A Handbook of Copyright Law (1999)

3.12 Copyright Act:

The Law on the subject is covered by the Copyright Act; the Trade and Merchandise Marks Act; Patents Act and the Designs Act. These are mainly based on the English law on the subject. The law is poised for fundamental changes to meet the international commitment of the Indian Government under the TRIPS/WTO Agreement.

In this article, we briefly describe the existing laws as well as the proposed changes.

Copyright

Copyright protection in India is available for any literary, dramatic, musical, sound recording and artistic work. The Copyright Act 1957 provides for registration of such works. Although an author's copyright in a work is recognised even without registration, it is advisable to get the same registered since it furnishes prima facie evidence of copyright in a court of law.

Infringement of copyright entitles the owner to remedies of injunction, damages and accounts.

Copyright in a literary, dramatic, musical or artistic work (other than a photograph) published within the lifetime of the author subsists for fifty years from the lifetime of the author. An Amendment Bill is on the anvil to extend the term in favour of performers[1] (at present twenty five years) to fifty years (in order to bring it in accord with the TRIPS Agreement). The amendment also aims to bring original works relating to satellite broadcasting, computer software and digital technology under copyright protection. With the issuance of the International Copyright Order, 1999,the provisions of Copyright Act have been extended to nationals of all World Trade Organization (WTO) Member countries.

Trade Marks

The law relating to registration of trade marks is governed by the Trade and Merchandise Marks Act, 1958. A distinctive mark (as defined) can be registered under the said Act. In case of infringement of registered trademarks, the statutory remedies of injunction, damages, accounts and delivery up of infringing labels and marks are available. An action for "passing-off" would lie in relation to an unregistered mark under certain circumstances.

In order to simplify the law and meet India's international obligations under the TRIPS, a new law called the Trade Marks Act, 1999 has been passed but has not yet been brought into force. Extensive changes have been introduced by the new Act. The major changes are given below:

- Definition of a 'mark' is extended to include the shape of goods, packaging, and combination of colours.

- Service Marks: These would now be allowed to be registered.

- Well Known 'Mark': An application for registration of a mark may be refused if it is similar or identical to a well known mark.

- Collective marks: The new Act will permit registration of marks in favour of associations of persons as "collective marks". Collective marks are defined as signs which distinguish the geographical origin, material, mode of manufacture, quality or other common characteristics of goods or services used or intended to be used, in commerce, by the members of a co-operative, an association, or other collective group or organisation.

- Duration of registration: The 7 years period available under the existing Act has been increased to 10 years, extendable by further periods of ten years each.

- Multiclass registration applications: Applicants would be able to file a single application for marks capable of registration in number of classes.

- Infringement of a mark: Offences relating to trade mark infringement have been dealt with more severely under the new Act.

Patents

The subject is covered by the Patents Act, 1970. India recognises product patent protection for a period of 14 years. However, in three areas: food, chemicals and pharmaceuticals, it recognises only a process patent for a period of 7 years. With the signing of the GATT Agreement, the Patents Act, 1970 has been amended by the Patents (Amendment) Act, 1999 to bring it in line with the Trade TRIPS Agreement. The amended law would allow the filing of all product patents with a regulatory authority. It also contains provision for granting Exclusive Marketing Rights (EMRs) for five years or till the patent is granted or rejected whichever is earlier.

The Patents (Second Amendment) Act 2002[2] recently passed by the Parliament provides protection for new micro organisms and proposes a uniform 20 year term from filing date for all patents granted after commencement of the Act. It also provides for publication of all patent applications within 18 months of filing or priority date, whichever is earlier.

Industrial Design

The Designs Act, 2000 protects certain designs. The features of shape, configuration, pattern, ornament or composition of lines or colours applied to any 'article' whether in two or three dimensional forms (or both), by an industrial process which appeals to the eye can be registered under the said Act. The Designs Act 2000 brought into force in May 2001 entitles an applicant to apply for registration in more than one class. However, registration is granted for only one class. Furthermore detailed classification of designs has been incorporated conforming to the international regime.Copyright in the design under the 2000 Act would be protected for a period of 10 years from the date of registration.

Geographical Indication

The Geographical Indication of Goods (Registration and Protection) Act, 1999, was enacted to register and protect geographical indicia of goods that originate from or are manufactured in a particular territory, region or even locality. These goods include agricultural, natural or manufactured goods that are distinct from similar products due to quality, reputation or any other characteristic that is essentially attributable to their geographical origin. Under the Act, such distinctive geographical indicia can be protected by registration. The Act thus facilitates promotion of Indian goods when exported overseas and in turn protects consumers from deception.

An application for registration of a geographical indication can be made by any authority, organization or association of persons representing the interest of the producers of the concerned goods. Registration would entitle a registered proprietor, or a duly authorized user, to the exclusive right of usage of that particular geographical indication with respect to the goods for which it is registered and to obtain relief for any infringement thereof. It may be pointed out however, that non-registration does not mean non-protection of a rightful user. Registration affords better protection in an action for infringement.

The validity of bona fide registration of a geographical indication as a trade mark prior to the coming into force of the Act will not be affected by this enactment and will be treated as valid under the laws relating to trade marks.

4. Information Security Controls

4.1 Input, process, validation, output, logical access, physical access.

4.2 Database, network, environment, BCP, DRP , Evidence collection, evaluation and Reporting Methodologies

Introduction:-

Definition of Controls: A control is any administrative, management, technical, or legal method that is used to manage risk. Controls aresafeguards or countermeasures.Controls includethingslike practices, policies, procedures, programs, techniques, technologies, guidelines, and organizational structures.

Information security policies are essential for managing a system, application and network. At the same time, controls are needed to enhance trust in the information systems and are put in place to protect the systems, applications network from attacks.

Security controls are protections orcountermeasures to avoid, counteract or diminishsecurityrisks relating to computersoftware, hardware, personal and organization assets. Organisation to organization or business-to-business facing enterprise whose service may affect the financial statements of the other enterprise, the prospect may require successful audit reports of policy controls.

Computer security is often divided into three distinct master categories, commonly referred to as controls:

- Common controls

- Technical controls

- Management controls

- Operational Controls

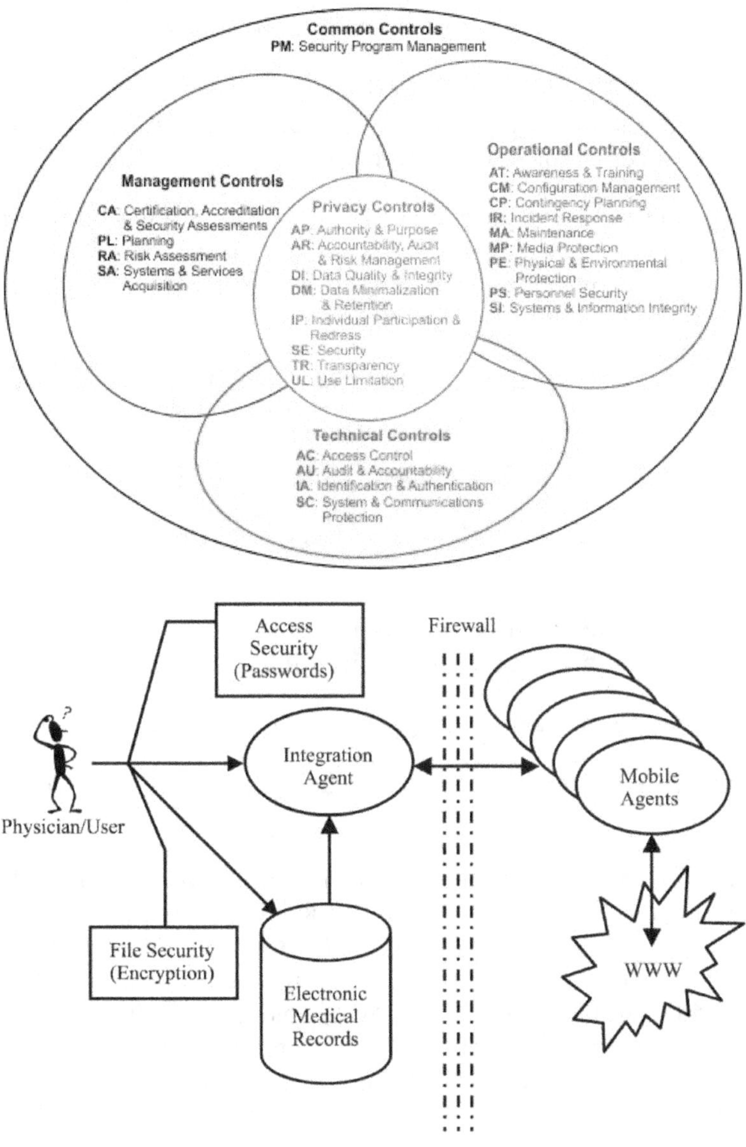

To design security controls, they can be classified by several criteria, for example according to the time that they act, relation to a security event:

- Before the incident, **preventive controls** are intended to prevent an incident from occurring e.g. by locking out unauthorized intruders;

- During the incident, **detective controls** are intended to identify and characterize an incident in progress e.g. by sounding the intruder alarm and alerting the security guards;

- After the incident, **corrective controls** are intended to limit the extent of any damage caused by the incident e.g. by recovering the organization to normal working status as efficiently as possible.

Security controls can also be categorized according to their nature, for example:

- **Physical controls** e.g. doors, locks and fire extinguishers;

- **Procedural controls** e.g. incident response processes, security awareness and training;

- **Technical controls** e.g. user authentication and logical access controls, antivirus software, firewalls;

- **Compliance controls** e.g. privacy laws, clauses and policies.

A similar categorization distinguishes control involving people, technology and processes.

Information security controls protect the **confidentiality**, **integrity** and **availability** of information (the so-called CIA Triangle). Risk-aware organizations may choose actively to specify, design, implement, maintain and operate their security controls, usually by assessing the risks and implementing a comprehensive security management framework such as **ISO/IEC 27002**. Organizations may also choose to demonstrate the adequacy of their information security controls by being independently assessed against certification standards such as **ISO/IEC 27001.**

Operational Controls-These controls must be defined, implemented, maintained, and include the following:

- System build and maintenance standards

- A change and configuration management process

- Backup and recovery processes for critical information and software

- A malicious code and unauthorized software countermeasure process

- Information security technical architecture standards

- A data protection and destruction process

- Secure development practices

- A business continuity and disaster recovery plan

- Acceptable use standards.

Technical Security &Access Controls -Technical security and access controls limit access to official information and systems in accordance with the organisation'sinformation security and privacy policies and standards. These controls must be defined, implemented, maintained, and include the following:

- Remote access process.

- An authentication mechanism for all authorized users and information systems.

- An access authorization process for all users and information systems.

- Network, system, and application level protection measures.

- Cryptographic controls for protecting data.

Monitoring Controls- Monitoring controls define the incident information that will be logged and monitored, and alert levels that will be triggered for event response.

These controls must be defined, implemented, maintained, and include the following:

- An intrusion detection mechanism

- A baseline measurement process for application, system, and network activity

- Logging processes for networks, systems, and applications.

- A monitoring capability for critical systems

Physical Controls-Physical controls define the protection required for the data center, physical assets, critical information systems.These controls must be defined, implemented, maintained, and include the following:

- A physical protection process for critical information systems and institutional information.

- Physical protection and access processes for buildings that house critical information technology and systems

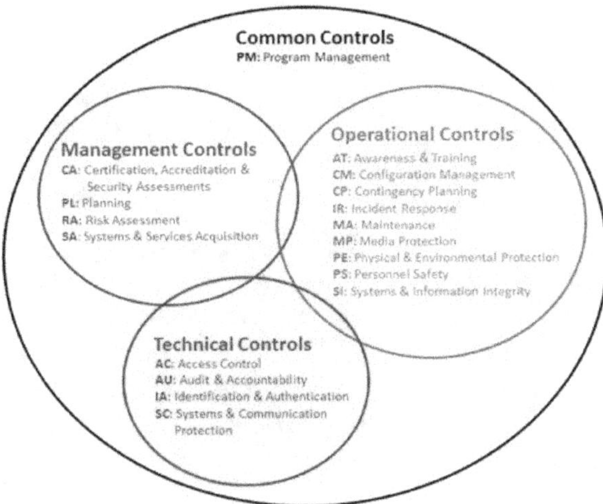

4.1.1 Input:

All information systems take some input and process it to produce output.Security controls are put into place to ensure that as data moves through thesystem it is processed correctly according to the protocols of the system.

e.g. i) Input security controls are to have a policy to allow only authorizedusers to input data.

ii) Input security control is to have the system validateall input. For example, if a name is put into the system, it should not contain special characters.

4.1.2 Process

Processing controls ensure that transactions are completed correctly. If processing is interrupted, processing controls ensure the system recovers and transactions are not left hanging. Output security controls guard who has access to the output and also guards the integrity of the output. An example output control is to allow printing only to certain printers in secure locations. Marking and numbering output copies is another control used to track and control distribution of sensitive output

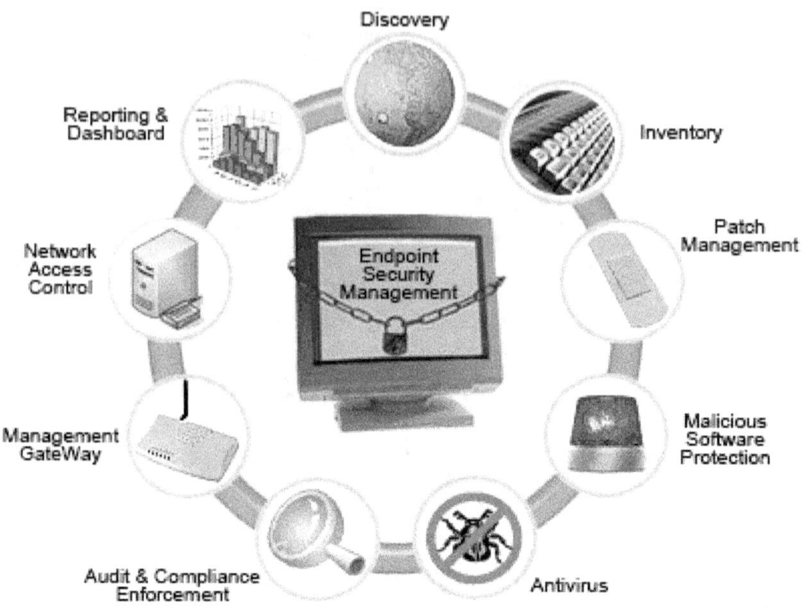

4.1.3 Validation

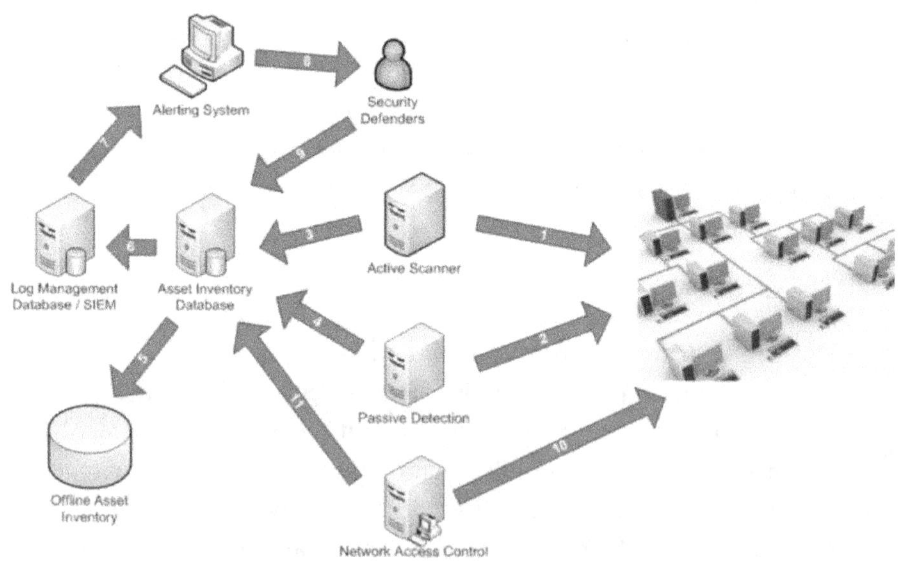

Policy Validation control

Program address select controls within the policies ,and are subject to assessments that –

Access Control - organizational and legal requirements, logical rights management, and privilege process for granting, modifying, and removing access

- **Antivirus** - Installation, configuration and update frequency requirements

- **Application Change Control** - Testing, patching, tracking and resolution

- **Back-Up** - complete backups, incremental backups, archive logs

- **Business Continuity / Disaster Recovery** - escalation, recovery, testing

- **Corrective Action** - compliance and enforcement with security policies and procedures

- **Data Breach Notification** - Communication process for informing affected individuals of security breaches exposing personal data

- **E-Mail** - Normal use, prohibitions,, message content restriction

- **Encryption** - When to use, roles and responsibilities

- **Firewall** - Access, authentication, routing,

- **Help Desk** - Creating and access, logging, training, logged data.

- **Incident Response** - Roles and responsibilities, detailed escalation procedures, disciplinary procedures, documentation and recovery procedures

- **Internet Usage** - Permitted use, monitoring, allowed services

- **Online Visitor Privacy** - Use of privacy statements

- **Passwords** - creation, protection, and reuse requirements for desktops, servers, applications.

- **Physical Security** - Physical access controls, response, , environmental requirements.

- **Wireless** - Approval, configuration, maintenance, and cryptography requirements

4.1.4 Logical access

Logical access controls are tools used for identification, authorization, authentication, and accountability in computerinformation systems. They are components that enforce access control measures for systems, programs, processes, and information.Logical access controls can be rooted within operating systems, applications, and database.

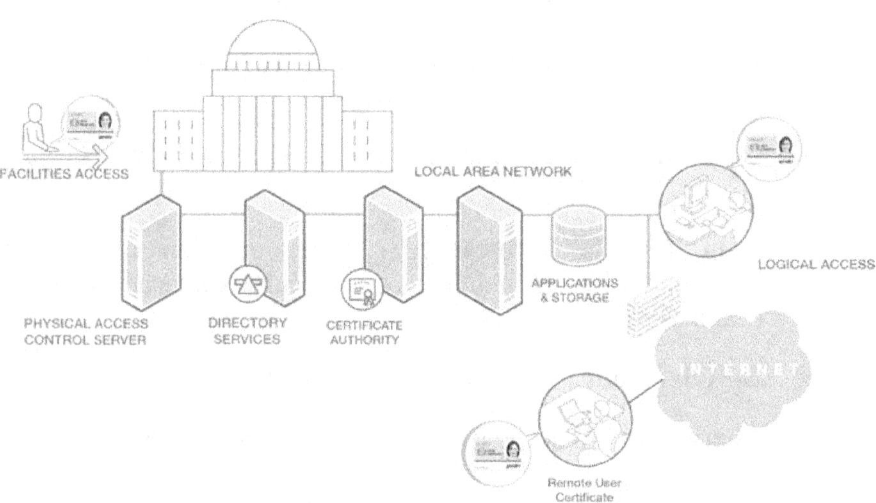

Logical access control can be contrasted with physical access control-but the line between the two can be unclear when physical access is controlled by software.

E.g. Entry to office may be controlled by a chip and PIN card and an electronic lock controlled by software. Only those in possession of an appropriate card, with an appropriate security level and with knowledge of the PIN are permitted entry to the office. On swiping the card into a card reader and entering the correct PIN, the user's security level is checked against a security database and compared to the security level required to enter the room. If the user meets the security requirements, entry is permitted. Having logical access controlled centrally in software allows a user's physical access permissions to be rapidly revised.

Logical Controls, may be called logical access controls and technical controls, protect data and the systems, networks, and environments that protect them. In order to authenticate, authorize, or maintain accountability a variety of methodologies are used such as password protocols, devices fixed with protocols and software, encryption, firewalls and maintain security, reduce vulnerabilities and protect the data and systems from threats.

4.1.5. Physical access

Physical security defines security measures that are designed to deny unauthorized access to facilities, assets and resources, and to protect property from damage Physical security contains the use of multiple layers of interdependent systems which include CCTV surveillance, security guards, protective locks, access control protocols, and many other techniques.

Physical security systems for protected facilities are generally proposed as-

- Prevent potential intruders

- Identify authorized from unauthorized people

- delay, disturb and ideally prevent intrusion attempts (e.g. strong walls, door locks)

- detect intrusions and record intruders (e.g. intruder alarms and CCTV systems)

- Activate appropriate incident responses (e.g. security guards and police).

4.2.1 Database

Database controls are best if you want to get in-utilize existing databases in their applications.

E.g. VB creates a temporary object called a recordset, which contains the data (rows and columns) from one or more tables in the database. The recordsetis not the database, it is just a working copyof some or part of the database tables.

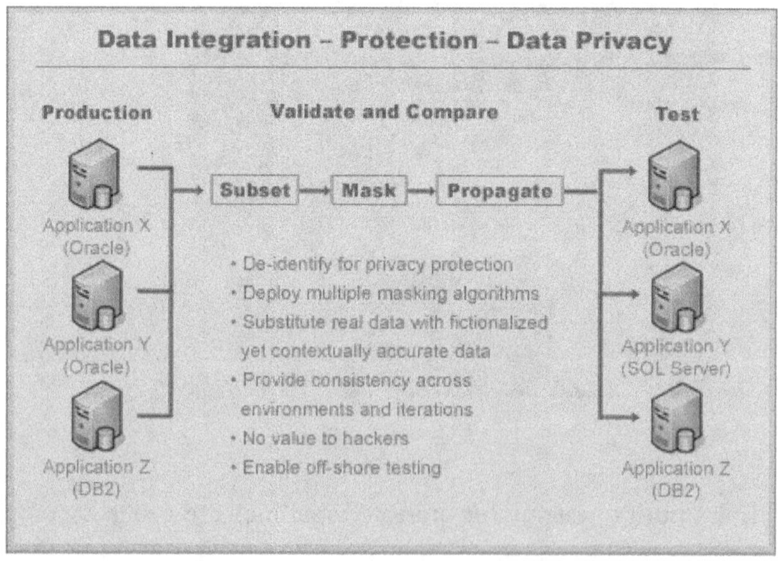

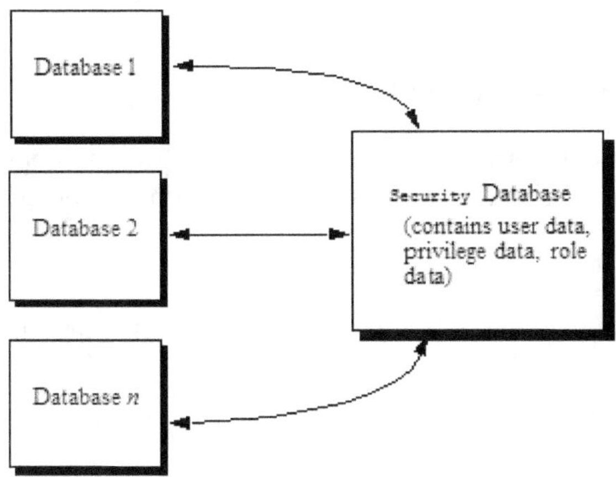

A recordset does not necessarily contain the entire contents of a table within a database file. You can use SQL queries to limit the recordset to selected records. Finally, you should understand that the records in a recordset are in no particular order unless you write code to order them.You can manipulate the contents of the recordset but the actual database file will not be changed until you or the user take action to save the changes.

DAO (Data Access Object)

The first method VB offered for using ODBC to create/edit databases was DAO. It allowed the programmer to create a variety of objects in code, objects whose properties and methods could be used by programmers to create/edit the databases.

VB Data Control

DataBaseName property to tell the data control which database file to read RecordSource property to tell it which table within the file to make available as a recordset to other controls.

For any controls which support databases, you set the .DataSource property to the data control and the .DataField property to the specific field within the table/record set that you want bound to the control.

Two data controls-

- **Data control (intrinsic version)**

  This is the original, intrinsic version of the control. It supports the JET database engine and can satisfy most beginners' needs.

- **ADO Data control**

  This is the latest version of the data control, implemented as an ActiveX control.

Data Bound Controls

Once you have the recordset available from the data control, you'll find VB to have a rich variety of controls which can access the recordset. There are 7 intrinsic controls and 16 ActiveX controls which you have available to use.

There are 8 intrinsic controls which can be bound to fields in a recordset:

- checkbox

- combobox

- data control

- image control

- label

- listbox

- picturebox

- textbox

There are also 16 ActiveX controls which can be bound to fields/recordsets:

- ADO Data control
- DataComboBox
- DataGrid
- DataList
- DataRepeater
- DateTimePicker
- DBCombo
- DBGrid
- DBList
- ImageCombo
- MaskedEdit
- MonthView
- MSChart
- MSHFlexGrid
- MSFlexGrid
- RichTextBox

4.2.2. Network

A control network is a network of nodes that jointlymonitor, accessand control or enable control of an environment for a particular purpose.

E.g. Many more control networks already exist in everyday life in refrigerators, traffic light controls, automobiles, and on shop floors. Control networks vary extremely in the number of nodes in the network and in their complexity. Unlike networks that people use to communicate with each other, control networks tend to be unseen. In the future, control networks are expected to become anvital aspect.

Communication between nodes in a control network may be master-slaveorpeer-to-peer. The nodes in some control networks contain three processors in one: two dedicated to moving data within the network and one for the specialized program associated with that node. This modularity makes it cheaper and faster to build new processors for control networks. Increasingly, control networks are being made from hardware and software components.

Network access control (NAC), also called network admission control, is a method of boosting the security of a proprietary network by restricting the availability of network resources to endpoint devices that comply with a defined security policy.

A traditional network access server (NAS) is a server that performs authentication and authorization functions for potential users by verifying login information. In addition to these functions, NAC restricts the data that each particular user can access, as well as implementing anti-threat applications such as firewalls, antivirus software and spyware-detection programs. NAC also regulates and restricts the things individual subscribers can do once they are connected. Several major networking and IT vendors have introduced NAC products.

4.2.3 Environment

The elements of a control environment for IT, aligned with the organization management viewpoint and operating style. These elements should include requirements regarding delivery of value from IT investments, integrity, ethical values, accountability and responsibility. The control environment should be based on a culture that supports value delivery whilst managing significant risks, encourages cross-divisional co-operation and teamwork, promotes compliance and continuous process improvement, and handles process deviations.

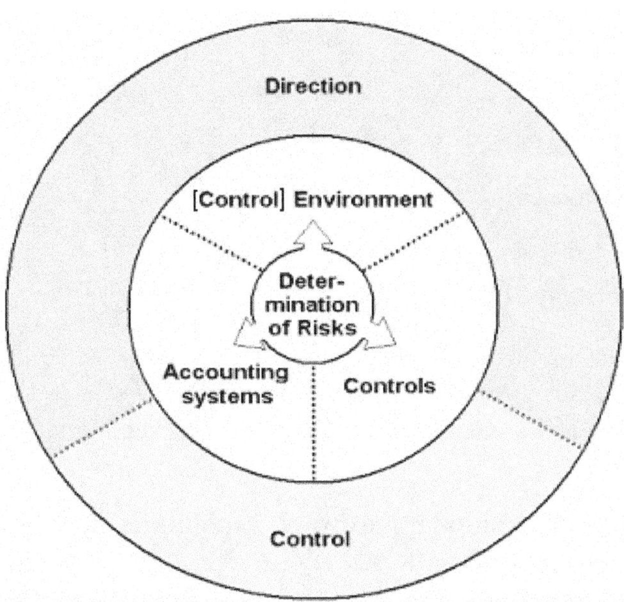

There should be need for policies and controls in a trusted environment. Many of network attacks succeed because policies are not properly implemented or trust mechanisms are compromised by the attackers.

Information security policies and controls for secure data transfer and storage that take advantage of trusted systems are developed.The main goal of policies and controls is to protect information systems. Managing security of information systems is essentially risk management, whichinvolves handling the threat of attacks on the system and dealing with the threat posed by known vulnerabilities.

Below digramdescribes exact scenarios in securing an information system:-

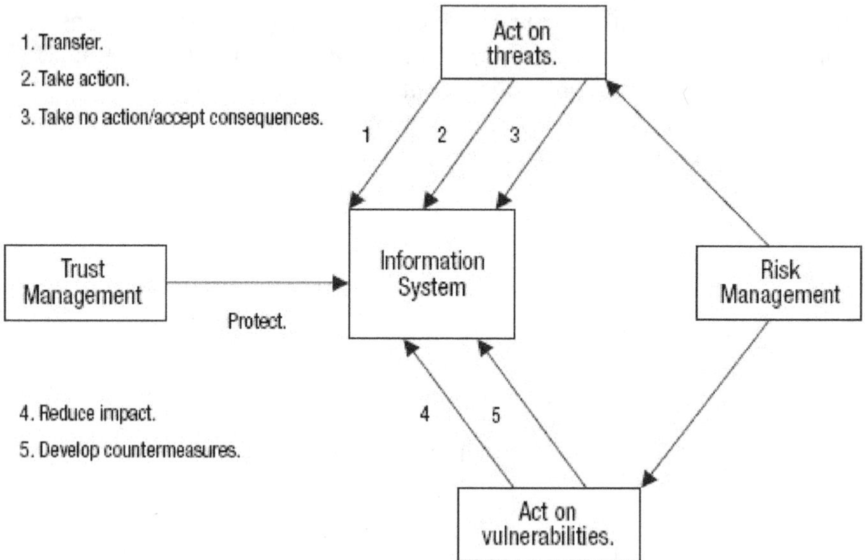

These policies and controls are considered for protecting an information system:

- **Policy 1: Validate hardware capabilities for secure data transfer and storage.**

- **Policy 2: Create role-based access privileges.**

- **Policy 3: Keep authorization and approval roles separate.**

- **Policy 4: Use public key infrastructure methods for secure communication.**

- **Policy 5: Use a trust score for nodes for participation in the organizational network.**

4.2.4 BCP – Business Continuity Plan

A Business Continuity Plan (BCP) / Disaster Recovery Plan (DRP) involves the creation of a plan for how an enterprise will recover and restore partially or completely interrupted crucial (risky) functions within a predetermined time after a disaster disruption.

These plans identify:-

- Required resources to support business continuity, including personnel, information, equipment, financial allocations, legal, infrastructure protection.

- Measures and monitor to ensure the continuous delivery of critical services and products, which permits the organization to recover its facility, data and assets.

4.2.5 Evidence Collection

A **"security incident"** as defined as security-relevantsystem event in which the system's security policy is disobeyed orbreached.The purpose of this document is to provideSystem Administrators with guidelines on the collection and archivingof evidence relevant to such a security incident. It's not ourintention to insist that all System Administrators rigidly followthese guidelines every time they have a security incident. Rather, we want to provide guidance on what they should do if they choose to collect and protect information relating to an intrusion.

Evidence is used to authenticate the code. As such there are several identity permissions that are used to identify code:

1. PublisherIdentityPermissionmodels the software publisher's digital signature. This answers the question: Who published the assembly?

2. SiteIdentityPermission models the web site where code originated. This answers the question: From what web site did the assembly come?

3. StrongNameIdentityPermission models the strong name of an assembly. This answers the question: What is the name of this assembly?

4. ZoneIdentityPermission models the zone where the code originated, corresponding to the Internet Explorer zones: Local intranet, Trusted sites, Internet, Restricted.

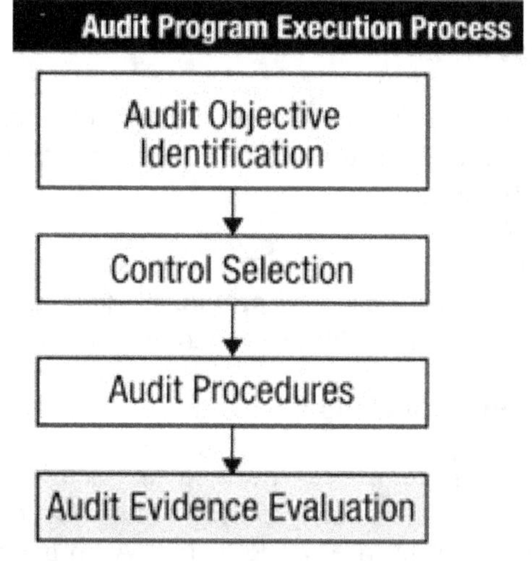

Controls, Evidence-gathering Techniques, Evidence Collected and Sampling Method			
Control	Evidence-gathering Technique	Evidence Collected	Sampling Method
Data owners authorize user access and user rights on the systems.	• Interview • Extraction of system parameters (automated/manual)	• User policy and procedure • User listing report with user creation dates • User access request form/emails showing management approval	Random selection
Users have unique IDs.	• Interviews of relevant IS personnel • Extraction of system parameters • Data interrogation	• User policy and procedure • User listing report from the system • ACL/IDEA report showing results obtained • Manual Excel sheet showing results obtained	Random sampling or an IS auditor performing a 100 percent review of the population by finding duplicate user IDs using CAATs (ACL/IDEA)
Systems are protected through strong passwords.	• Interviews • Extraction of system parameters	• User policy and procedure • System configuration/screen prints for the password policy	No sampling, as this is an automated control (As noted previously, additional testing may be required on some systems.)
Privileged roles (administrator) have been granted to appropriate personnel.	Extraction of system parameters	• Policies and procedures • User listing/role reports • Job descriptions	• A 100 percent review of the population by extracting users with administrator rights using CAATs (ACL/IDEA) • Random sampling

Such collection represents a considerable effort on the part of theSystem Administrator.Bigprogress has been made in recent yearsto speed up the re-installation of the Operating System and tofacilitate the reversion of a system to a 'known' state, thus makingthe 'easy option' even more attractive. Meanwhile little has beendone to provide easy ways of archiving evidence. Further, increasing disk and memory capacities and the morewidespread use of stealth and cover-your-tracks tactics by attackershave exacerbated the problem.If evidence collection is done correctly, it is much more useful inapprehending the attacker, and stands a much greater chance of beingadmissible in the event of a prosecution.

You should use these guidelines as a basis for formulating yoursite's evidence collection procedures, and should incorporate yoursite's procedures into your Incident Handling documentation. Theguidelines in this document may not be appropriate under alljurisdictions. Once you've formulated your site's evidencecollection procedures, you should have law enforcement for yourjurisdiction confirm that they're adequate.

Principles during Evidence Collection

Adhere to your site's Security Policy and engage theappropriate Incident Handling and Law Enforcement personnel.

- Keep detailed notes. These should include dates and times. Ifpossible generate an automatic transcript.Notes and print-outs should be signed and dated.

- Note the difference between the system clock and UTC. For each

- Time stamp provided, indicate whether UTC or local time is used.

- Remove external avenues for change.

- Be prepared to testify (perhaps years later) outlining allactions you took and at what times. Detailed notes will bevital.

- Minimise changes to the data as you are collecting it.This isnot limited to content changes; you should avoid updating fileor directory access times.

- Capture as accurate a picture of the system as possible.

- When confronted with a choice between collection and analysisyou should do collection first and analysis later.

- For each device, a methodical approach should be adopted whichfollows the guidelines laid down in your collection procedure. Speed will often be critical so where there are a number ofdevices requiring examination it may be appropriate to spreadthe work among your team to collect the evidence in parallel.However on a single given system collection should be done stepby step.

- Proceed from the volatile to the less volatile.

- Though it hardly needs stating, your procedures should be implementable. As with any aspect of an incident response policy, procedures should be tested to ensure feasibility, particularly in a crisis. If possible procedures should be automated for reasons of speed and accuracy. Be methodical.

Collection Procedure

Your collection procedures should be as detailed as possible. As isthe case with your overall Incident Handling procedures, they shouldbe unambiguous, and should minimise the amount of decision-makingneeded during the collection process.

Collection Steps

Where is the evidence? List what systems were involved in theincident and from which evidence will be collected.

- Establish what is likely to be relevant and admissible. Whenin doubt error on the side of collecting too much rather than notenough.

- For each system, obtain the relevant order of volatility.

- Remove external avenues for change.

- Document each step.

- Don't forget the people involved. Make notes of who was thereand what were they doing, what they observed and how theyreacted.

- Record the extent of the system's clock drift.

- Question what else may be evidence as you work through the collection steps.

4.2.6 Evaluation and Reporting methodologies

Policy heads are responsible for monitoring compliance with the policy in their departments to ensure its effective implementation. They are responsible for ensuring that a neutral assessment of their departmental evaluation function is conducted.Also responsible for addressing issues that arise regarding compliance with the policy, and with its associated directive and standard, and ensuring that appropriate remedial actions are taken to address these issues.

The use of evaluation in support of the requirements of the management system, including the extent to which evaluation information is used within the department:

1. To manage for results and inform resource reallocation decisions;

2. To provide evidence for use in strategic reviews of program spending;

3. To support accountability, including through public reporting.

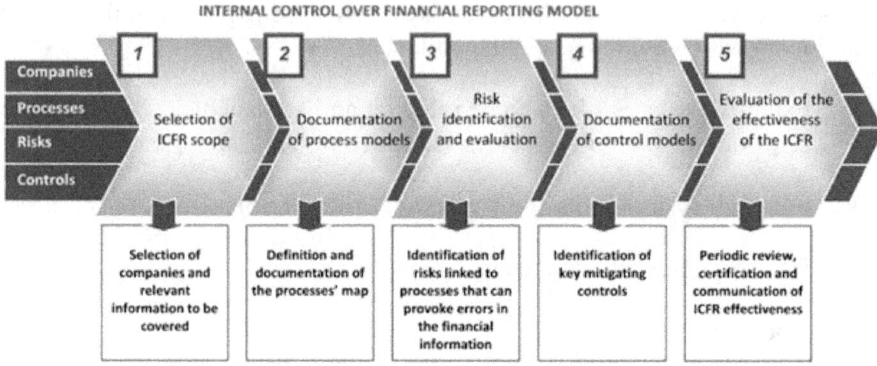

5. Auditing Concepts

5.1. Security Audits what are they?

5.2. Need for Security audits in organizations

5.3. Auditors responsibility in Security audits

5.4. Types of Audits & approaches to Audits Technology based Audits

5.5. Vulnerability scanning and penetration testing

5.6. Resistance to Audits

5.7. Key success factors for Security Audits

5.1. Security Audits what are they?

An information system is not just a computer. Today's information systems are complex and have many components that piece together to make a business solution. Assurances about an information system can be obtained only if all the components are evaluated and secured.

Information Systems Security Audit is an independent review and examination of system records, activities and related documents to determine the adequacy of system controls, ensure compliance with established security policy and approved operational procedures, detect breaches in security so as to verify whether data integrity is maintained, assets are safeguarded, organizational goals are achieved effectively and resources are used efficiently. Security audit is a systematic, measurable technical assessment of how security policies are built into the information systems.

Auditing is a systematic and independent examination of information systemsenvironment to ascertain whether the objectives, set out to be achieved, have been metor not. Auditing is also described as a continuous search for compliance. The objectiveof the IS audit are to identify risks that an organization is exposed to in the computerizedenvironment. IS audit evaluates the adequacy of the security controls and informs themanagement with suitable conclusions and recommendations. IS audit is anindependent subset of the normal audit exercise. Information systems audit is anongoing process of evaluating controls; suggest security measures for the purpose ofsafeguarding assets/resources, maintaining data integrity, improve system effectivenessand system efficiency for the purpose of attaining organization goals. Well-planned andstructured audit is essential for risk management and monitoring and control ofinformation systems in any organization.

An information security audit is an audit on the level of information security in an organization. Within the broad scope of auditing information security there are multiple types of audits, multiple objectives for different audits, etc. Most commonly the controls being audited can be categorized –

- Technical

- Physical

- Administrative

Auditing information security covers topics from auditing the physical security of data centers to auditing the logical security of databases and highlights key components to look for and different methods for auditing these areas.

When centered on the IT aspects of information security, it can be seen as a part of an information technology audit. It is often then referred to as an information technology security audit or a computer security audit. However, information security encompasses much more than IT.

Audit Objectives

Auditing is a systematic and independent examination of information systemsenvironment to ascertain whether the objectives, set out to be achieved, have been metor not. Auditing is also described as a continuous search for compliance. The objectiveof the IS audit are to identify risks that an organization is exposed to in the computerizedenvironment. IS audit evaluates the adequacy of the security controls and informs themanagement with suitable conclusions and recommendations. IS audit is anindependent subset of the normal audit exercise. Information systems audit is anongoing process of evaluating controls; suggest security measures for the purpose ofsafeguarding assets/resources, maintaining data integrity, improve system effectivenessand system efficiency for the purpose of attaining organization goals. Well-planned andstructured audit is essential for risk management and monitoring and control of information systems in any organization.

5.2. Need for Security audits in organizations:

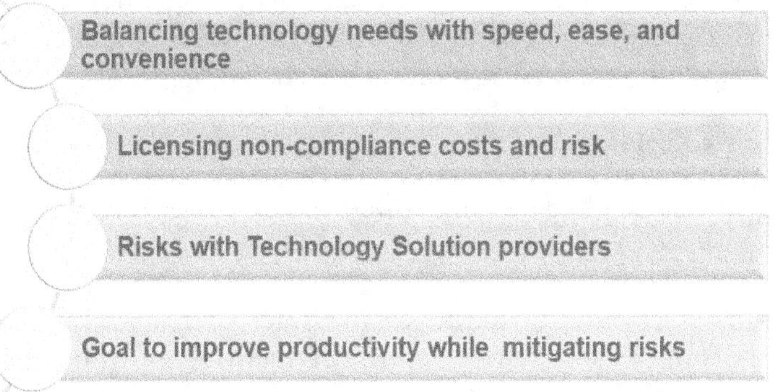

To ensure that the security is in order to ensure that organizations security systems and processes are working as intended

•To verify and ensure compliance with some the legislations and acts

•To identify the gaps in the existing defenses.

Over the past few of years, OIL has used IT as a means of increasing operational efficiencies and as a business driver. Consequentially, the company has invested substantially in areas such as:

- IT infrastructure

- Line building

- Implementing ERP systems

- E-mail

- Other workflow applications

As an increasing number of people were gaining access to business critical resources through the growing use of information technology, security became a real concern for the top management.

When the management chose to beat competition by giving employees increased access to business critical resources, it also felt the need to conduct a security audit to get a closer look at the strengths and weaknesses of the current infrastructure along with advice on strategies and policies required to stay competitive.

OIL chose Sify as its auditor. "Since they already were our Internet bandwidth service provider, we felt that they could provide us with world-class network security services as well," said A.K. Sircar, Controller - Information Technology, for the company.

The audit solution

The audit was divided into three phases: Assessment, Supply & Deployments, and Review.

Most businesses are connected to the Internet and have implemented measures (policies, systems) to protect themselves from unauthorized access/transactions

- IT can be at risk, even with all the right technology, if security policy and proceduresare Poorly implemented or outdated

- A few software vulnerabilities account for majority of successful attacks

- Hackers/attackers are opportunistic – taking the easiest and most convenient route.

- Hacking exploits the best-known flaws with the most effective and widely availableattack tools

- It counts on organizations not fixing the problems, and they often attackindiscriminately, by scanning the Internet for vulnerable systems

Information security organizations and audit organizations have the same goal: to see that mission-critical information is properly protected from unauthorized access and/or update. It is wise for security practitioners to bring audit guidance into a security project -- to include deploying firewalls and intrusion detection systems -- during the early planning stages. This will help to ensure that the resulting controls will be appropriately implemented, both technically and operationally, for protection as well as compliance with security policies that govern the overall security program

In the early days of computers, many people were suspicious of their ability to replace human beings performing complex tasks. The first business software applications were mostly in the domain of finance and accounting. The numbers from paper statements and receipts were entered into the computer, which would perform calculations and create reports. Computers were audited using sampling techniques. An auditor would collect the original paper statements and receipts, manually perform the calculations used to create each report, and compare the results of the manual calculation with those generated by the computer. In the early days, accountants would often find programming errors, and these were computer audit findings.

As computers became more sophisticated, auditors recognized that they had fewer and fewer findings related to the correctness of calculations and more and more on the side of unauthorized access. Moreover, the checks and balances that were devised to maintain correctness of calculations were implemented as software change control measures.

These rely heavily on security to enforce controls over segregation of duties between programming, testing, and deployment staff. This meant that even programming changes relied in some measure for their effectiveness on computer security controls. Nowadays, information systems audit seems almost synonymous with information security control testing.

The Scope of an IS Audit:

However, the normal scope of an information systems audit still does cover the entire lifecycle of the technology under scrutiny, including the correctness of computer calculations. The word "scope" is prefaced by "normal" because the scope of an audit is dependent on its objective. Audits are always a result of some concern over the management of assets. The concerned party may be a regulatory agency, an asset owner, or any stakeholder in the operation of the systems environment, including systems managers themselves. That party will have an objective in commissioning the audit. The objective may be validating the correctness of the systems calculations, confirming that systems are appropriately accounted for as assets, assessing the operational integrity of an automated process, verifying that confidential data is not exposed to unauthorized individuals, and/or multiple combinations of these and other systems-related matters of importance. The objective of an audit will determine its scope.

IS Audit Standards:

Standards provide the information required to meet the compliance needs of IS audit and assurance professionals, as well as providing essential guidance to improve effectiveness and efficiency. IS standards enables IS audit and assurance professionals to approach their challenges with a risk-based approach that is aligned with **IS** methodology.

The purpose of this IS Auditing Standard is to establish and provide guidance regarding the Audit Charter used during the audit process.

IS Audit and Assurance Standards apply to individuals who act in the capacity of IS audit and assurance professionals and are engaged in providing assurance over some components of IS systems, applications and infrastructure. However, these standards, guidelines, and IS audit and assurance procedures have been designed in a manner that may also be useful, and provide benefits to, a wider audience, including users of IS audit and assurance reports.

- The IS auditor should, where appropriate, consider using the work of other experts for the audit.

- The IS auditor should assess and be satisfied with the professional qualifications, competencies, relevant experience, resources, independence and quality control processes of other experts, prior to engagement.

- The IS auditor should assess, review and evaluate the work of other experts as part of the audit and conclude the extent of use and reliance on expert's work.

- The IS auditor should determine and conclude whether the work of other experts is adequate and complete to enable the IS auditor to conclude on the current audit objectives. Such conclusion should be clearly documented.

- The IS auditor should apply additional test procedures to gain sufficient and appropriate audit evidence in circumstances where the work of other experts does not provide sufficient and appropriate audit evidence.

- The IS auditor should provide appropriate audit opinion and include scope limitation where required evidence is not obtained through additional test procedures.

GLBA   FISMA   HIPAA   BASEL II

SOX   Compliance Standards   FDCC

PCI-DSS   ISAP   CIS Benchmarks

COBIT   FIPS-199   DISA STIGs

The **British Standards Institution** (BSI) has recently updated its standards for information security auditing.

BSI recently updated ISO 27006, which provides minimum requirements for auditor competency for bodies that provide audit and certification of **information security management systems** (ISMS).

The **ISACA** goal is to advance globally applicable standards that address the specialized nature of IS audit and assurance and the skills necessary to perform such audits. **ISACA's** development and dissemination of the IS Audit and Assurance Standards are a cornerstone of its professional contribution to the audit and assurance community. The framework for the IS Audit and Assurance Standards provides multiple levels of guidance.

IS Audit and Assurance Standards apply to individuals who act in the capacity of IS audit and assurance professionals and are engaged in providing assurance over some components of IS systems, applications and infrastructure. However, these standards, guidelines, and IS audit and assurance procedures have been designed in a manner that may also be useful, and provide benefits to, a wider audience, including users of IS audit and assurance reports.

The objective of the IS Auditing Guidelines is to provide further information on how to comply with the IS Auditing Standards.

Performance

Performance auditmentions to an examination of a program, operation, functionor the management procedures and systems of a governmental or other enterprise to assess whether the entity is achieving economy, efficiency and effectiveness in the employment of available resources. The examination is objective and systematic, generally using structured and professionally adopted methodologies.

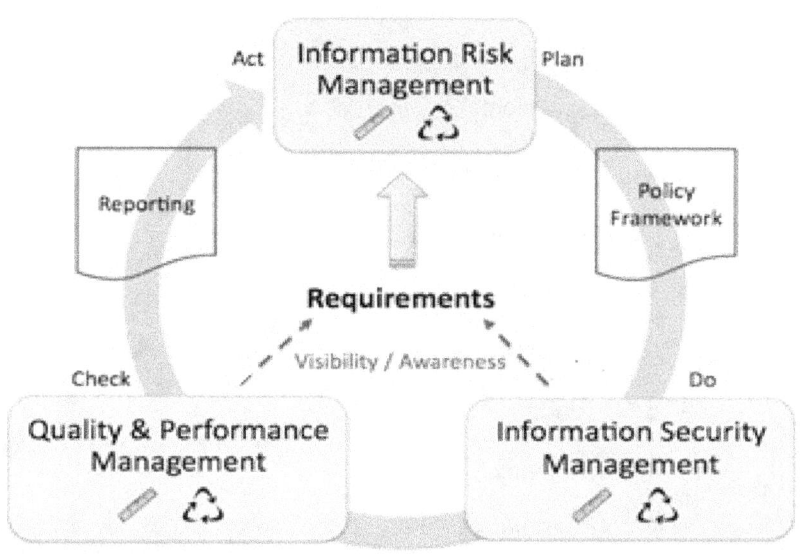

Performance audits of governmental activities are carried out by the external audit bodies. Many of these audit bodies have established guides for conducting performance audits which explain how performance audits are planned, conducted and its results reported.

Performance audits may also be conducted by Internal Auditors who are employees of the entity being audited. However, some national governments require agencies, departments and branches to periodically retain outside auditors to conduct them.

The scope of performance audits may include the detection of fraud, waste and abuse, although often these are not included in the scope. Prior to engaging in a performance audit, the auditor must have a scope and plan defined which will be used to guide the audit process.

Performance auditing differs from performance measurement, the latter being the responsibility of management of the entity. In addition, performance measurement may include a broad variety of activities that do not meet the rigour of an independent external assessment.

Definition of Performance auditing -"Performance auditing is an assessment of the activities of an organization to see if the resources are being managed with due regard for economy, efficiency and effectiveness and accountability requirements are being met reasonably."

It covers key words as:

1. assessment

2. organization

3. management

4. activities

5. resources

6. economy

7. efficiency

8. effectiveness

1. **Assessment:** It means that the auditor formulates a judgment on the basis of relevant and reliable evidence.

2. **Organization:** Performance auditing takes an over view of the activities and functions of an organization as a whole.

3. **Management:** Management covers such functions as planning, organization, resourcing, directing and controlling. Performance auditing reviews all these phases of management cycle.

4. **Activities:** Performance auditing extends to financial as well as non-financial activities of an organization.

5. **Resources:** The resources of an organization consist of money, men, materials, and machines. Performance auditing reviews all these resources.

6. **Economy:** Review of economy is a primary element in performance auditing. Economy means *acquiring* resources at the lowest cost keeping in view the objectives of the organization.

7. **Efficiency:** Efficiency refers to the relationship of inputs and outputs. It relates to utilization of resource.

8. **Effectiveness:** It means the extent to which an organization achieves its objectives.

INTOSAI, the international association of Supreme Audit Institutions, has published generally accepted principles of performance auditing in its implementation guidelines. In the United States, the standard for government performance audits is the **Generally Accepted Government Auditing Standards** (GAGAS), often referred to as the "yellow book", maintained by the federal **Government Accountability Office** (GAO). Similarly, the **European Court of Auditors** (ECA) has developed a "performance audit manual" for its audits of the sound financial management of the European Commission and the programmes funded through the EU budget.

IS Auditing Steps

Information systems audit is a part of the overall audit process, which is one of the facilitators for good corporate governance. While there is no single universal definition of IS audit, Ron Weber has defined it as "the process of collecting and evaluating evidence to determine whether a computer system (information system) safeguards assets, maintains data integrity, achieves organizational goals effectively and consumes resources efficiently."

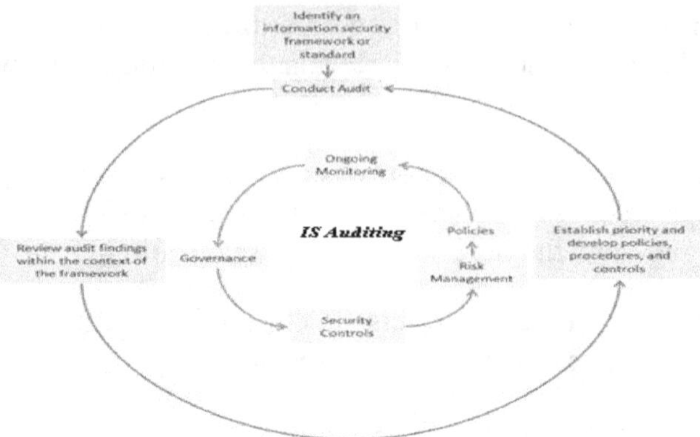

The purpose of IS audit is to review and provide feedback, assurances and suggestions. These concerns can be grouped under three broad heads:

1. **Availability:** Will the information systems on which the business is heavily dependent be available for the business at all times when required? Are the systems well protected against all types of losses and disasters?

2. **Confidentiality**: Will the information in the systems be disclosed only to those who have a need to see and use it and not to anyone else?

3. **Integrity**: Will the information provided by the systems always be accurate, reliable and timely? What ensures that no unauthorized modification can be made to the data or the software in the systems?

Key Challenge:-

IS audit often involves finding and recording observations that are highly technical. Such technical depth is required to perform effective IS audits. At the same time it is necessary to translate audit findings into vulnerabilities and businesses impacts to which operating managers and senior management can relate. Therein lies a main challenge of IS audit.

When the IS auditor becomes aware of information concerning a possible illegal act, the IS auditor should consider taking the following steps:

1. Obtain an understanding of the nature of the act.
2. Understand the circumstances in which it occurred.

3. Obtain sufficient supportive information to evaluate the effect of the irregularity or illegal act.
4. Perform additional procedures to determine the effect of the irregularity or illegal act and whether additional acts exist

The steps that can be followed for a risk-based approach to making an audit plan are:

1. Inventory the information systems in use in the organization and categorize them.

2. Determine which of the systems impact critical functions or assets, such as money, materials, customers, decision making, and how close to real time they operate.

3. Assess what risks affect these systems and the severity of impact on the business.

4. Rank the systems based on the above assessment and decide the audit priority, resources, schedule and frequency.

Elements of IS Audit:

The major elements of IS audit can be broadly classified:

1. **Physical and environmental review**—this includes physical security, power supply, air conditioning, humidity control and other environmental factors.

2. **System administration review**—this includes security review of the operating systems, database management systems, all system administration procedures and compliance.

3. **Application software review**—the business application could be payroll, invoicing, a web-based customer order processing system or an enterprise resource planning system that actually runs the business. Review of such application software includes access control and authorizations, validations, error and exception handling, business process flows within the application software and complementary

manual controls and procedures. Additionally, a review of the system development lifecycle should be completed.

4. **Network security review**—Review of internal and external connections to the system, perimeter security, firewall review, router access control lists, port scanning and intrusion detection are some typical areas of coverage.

5. **Business continuity review**—this includes existence and maintenance of fault tolerant and redundant hardware, backup procedures and storage, and documented and tested disaster recovery/business continuity plan.

6. **Data integrity review**—the purpose of this is scrutiny of live data to verify adequacy of controls and impact of weaknesses, as noticed from any of the above reviews. Such substantive testing can be done using generalized audit software

All these elements need to be addressed to present to management a clear assessment of the system. For example, application software may be well designed and implemented with all the security features, but the default super-user password in the operating system used on the server may not have been changed, thereby allowing someone to access the data files directly. Such a situation negates whatever security is built into the application. Likewise, firewalls and technical system security may have been implemented very well, but the role definitions and access controls within the application software may have been so poorly designed and implemented that by using their user IDs, employees may get to see critical and sensitive information far beyond their roles.

It is important to understand that each audit may consist of these elements in varying measures; some audits may scrutinize only one of these elements or drop some of these elements. While the fact remains that it is necessary to do all of them, it is not mandatory to do all of them in one assignment. The skill sets required for each of these are different. The results of each audit need to be seen in relation to the other. This will enable the auditor and management to get the total view of the issues and problems. This overview is critical.

IS Auditing Techniques:

IS Auditing technique is defined as any technique used by auditors to determine deviations from actual accounting and controls established by a business or organization as well as uncovering problems in established processes and controls. Auditing techniques can be used to aid organizations by uncovering errors in business practices and providing a means of correction. Some businesses have used irregular accounting methods to hide certain monetary transactions and non-compliant behavior which has been uncovered by the use of varied auditing techniques. Other businesses have found new ways to save money and streamline business practices through various auditing techniques which have found waste in certain processes.

Auditing techniques can be used to uncover these issues in order to ensure ethical business practices and to minimize waste within an organization. The applied techniques can determine if any income is hidden or improperly categorized or reported; transactions are being completed between the organization and regulated or prohibited persons, groups, or countries; uncovering of environmental waste discrepancies; finding of data inconsistencies; or any other business practice that can be considered as a process error, oversight, or violation of ethics, regulations, and laws.

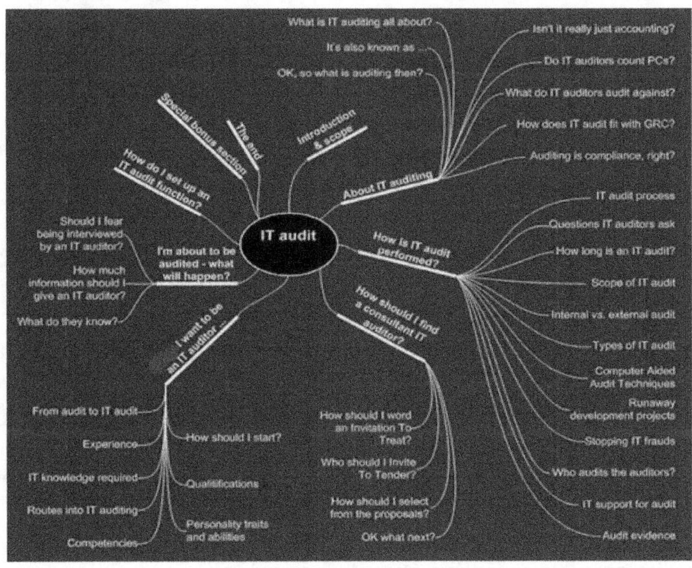

IS Auditing Methodology:

Methodology has been developed in accordance with International Information Systems Audit Standards e.g. ISACA Information Systems Audit Standards and Guidelines. The beginning point of this methodology is to carry out planning activities that are driving towards integrating a Risk Based Audit Approach to the IS Audit.

Phase 1: Audit Planning -In this phase we plan the information system coverage to comply with the audit objectives specified by the Client and ensure compliance to all Laws and Professional Standards. The first thing is to obtain an Audit Charter from the Client detailing the purpose of the audit, the management responsibility, authority and accountability of the Information Systems Audit function as follows:

1. Responsibility: The Audit Charter should define the mission, aims, goals and objectives of the Information System Audit. At this stage we also define the Key Performance Indicators and an Audit Evaluation process;

2. Authority: The Audit Charter should clearly specify the Authority assigned to the Information Systems Auditors with relation to the Risk Assessment work that will be carried out, right to access the Client's information, the scope and/or limitations to the scope, the Client's functions to be audited and the auditee expectations; and

3. Accountability: The Audit Charter should clearly define reporting lines, appraisals, assessment of compliance and agreed actions.

Phase 2: Risk Assessment and Business Process Analysis -Risk is the possibility of an act or event occurring that would have an adverse effect on the organization and its information systems. Risk can also be the potential that a given threat will exploit vulnerabilities of an asset or group of assets to cause loss of, or damage to, the assets. It is ordinarily measured by a combination of effect and likelihood of occurrence.

The process of quantifying risk is called Risk Assessment. Risk Assessment is useful in making decisions such as:

1. The area/business function to be audited

2. The nature, extent and timing of audit procedures

3. The amount of resources to be allocated to an audit

Control Risk:

Control risk is the risk that an error which could occur in an audit area, and which could be material, individually or in combination with other errors, will not be prevented or detected and corrected on a timely basis by the internal control system.

Detection Risk:

Detection risk is the risk that the IS auditor's substantive procedures will not detect an error which could be material, individually or in combination with other errors. In determining the level of substantive testing required, the IS auditor should consider both:

- The assessment of inherent risk

- The conclusion reached on control risk following compliance testing

The higher the assessment of inherent and control risk the more audit evidence the IS auditor should normally obtain from the performance of substantive audit procedures.

Below listed are some methodologies

- CobiT

- BS 7799 - Code of Practice (CoP)

- BSI - IT Baseline Protection Manual

- ITSEC

- Common Criteria (CC)

- CobiT: Audit method for all IT processes

- ITSEC, CC: Systematic approach for evaluations

- ■ BS7799, BSI: List of detailed security measures to be used as best practice documentation

Detailed audit plans, checklists, tools for technical audits (operating systems, LANs, etc.)

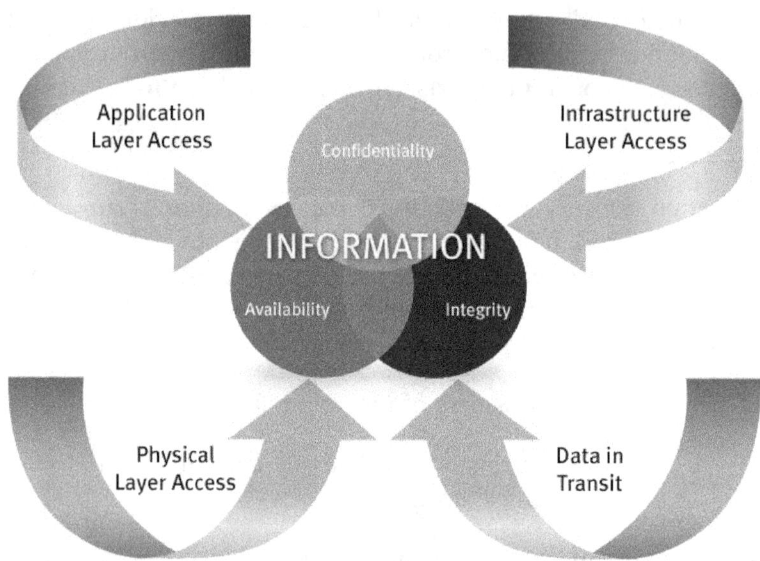

Audit Universe we perform the following:

- Identify areas where the risk is unacceptably high

- Identify critical control systems that address high inherent risks

- Assess the uncertainty that exists in relation to the critical control systems

In carrying out the Business Process Analysis:

- Obtain an understanding of the Client Business Processes

- Map the Internal Control Environment

- Identify areas of Control Weaknesses

Around and Through Auditing:

The risk-based audit approach starts with the preliminary review. The next step is riskassessment. Under the audit approach, depending upon the intensity of the use ofInformation Technology, audit is done either **through** the computers or **around** thecomputers. Once the approach is decided, the next step is to assess general IS controlsand application controls. Using (Use of Computer Assisted Audit Techniques) **CAATs**, the controls are assessed, evidence is collected, evaluated and reports are prepared using the information systems.

At this point it can be concluded that the auditor should audit around the computer. The reasons for this are firstly the applications are relative straightforward and simple. Second, it is more cost effective to audit around the computer when a generalize application software is being used. The application software was provided by a reputable vendor and is well tested, and the application has not been modified according to the general manager. Thirdly, since the package is well tested a high reliance is placed on user controls rather than computer controls. Thus there is no need to go through testing of processing logic and control in an application that is already tested by the vendor. This would require technical expertise to duplicate a task performed by a reputable vendor.

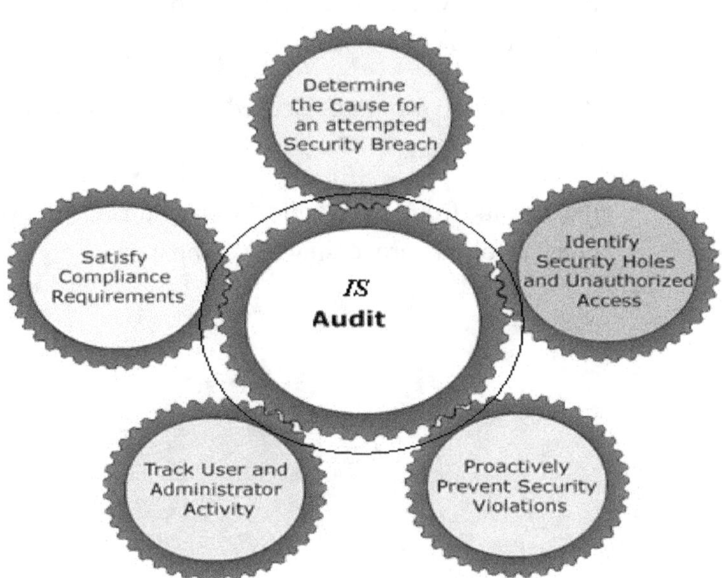

There are two general approaches to auditing systems:

1. Auditing "around" the computer involves extensive testing of the inputs andoutputs of the EDP system and little or no testing of processing or computer hardware. This approach involves no tests of thecomputer programs and no auditor useof the computer. Auditing **"around"** the computer depends on a visible, traceable, hard copy audit trail made of manually prepared and computer-prepared documents.

2. Auditing with use of the computer involves extensive testing of computer hardware and software.

Techniques for auditingwith use of the computer:

1. Test data involves auditor preparation of a series of fictitious transactions; many of those transactions will contain intentional errors. The auditor examines the results and determines whether the errors were detected by the client's system.

2. Parallel simulation:

- the auditor writes a computer program that replicates part of the client's system

- the auditor's program is used to process actual client data

- the results from the auditor's program and that of the client's routine processing are compared

5.3. Auditors responsibility in Security audits:

1	Define Roles & Responsibilities	Define the necessary Roles & Responsibilities including full time security personnel, Virtual Teams (for example, Incident Management) etc.
2	Define Policies	The Necessary Policies reflect the Legal, Regulatory and Stautory Requirements of the laws the entity is regulated under i.e. SOX, HIPAA, GLBA, PCIS, SB1386 etc. combined with best practices.
3	Identify All Data at Rest and in Transit	Identify all locations of data at rest and data in transit. Then isolate what data stores or transmissions contain data that requires special handling.
4	Development of Standards	a) Standards Development & Maintenance Program
5	Development of Procedures	b) Access Control & Identity Management c) Employee Awareness & Training Program d) Physical Environment Security e) Application Security, Development & Change Control
6	Awareness & Training	f) Contingency Planning (BCP & DR) g) Risk Assessment & Management Program h) Vulnerability Management & Software Maintenance Program
7	Auditing & Monitoring	i) Asset Identification, Control & Maintenance Program j) Incident Identification & Handling Program

A Security Auditor probes the safety and effectiveness of computer systems and their related security components.

After conducting a security audit, you will issue a detailed report that outlines the effectiveness of the system, explains any security issues and suggests changes and improvements.

Security Auditor Responsibilities:

In this mid-level role, you may be required to:

- Plan, execute and lead security audits across an organization

- Inspect and evaluate financial and information systems, management procedures and security controls

- Evaluate the efficiency, effectiveness and compliance of operation processes with corporate security policies and related government regulations

- Develop and administer risk-focused exams for IT systems

- Review or interview personnel to establish security risks and complications

- Execute and properly document the audit process on a variety of computing environments and computer applications

- Assess the exposures resulting from ineffective or missing control practices

- Accurately interpret audit results against defined criteria

- Weigh the relevancy, accuracy and perspective of conclusions against audit evidence

- Provide a written and verbal report of audit findings

- Develop rigorous "best practice" recommendations to improve security on all levels

- Work with management to ensure security recommendations comply with company procedure

- Collaborate with departments to improve security compliance, manage risk and bolster effectiveness

- Travel extensively

Hard Skills:

Wherever and whenever you can, gain experience in auditing computer applications and information systems of varying complexity. Employers may also specify a working knowledge of:

- Working knowledge of regulatory and industry data security standards (e.g. FFIEC, HIPAA, PCI, NERC, SOX, NIST, EU/Safe Harbor and GLBA)

- ISO 27001/27002, ITIL and COBIT frameworks

- Windows, UNIX and Linux operating systems

- MSSQL and ORACLE databases

- C, C++, C#, Java and/or PHP programming languages

- ACL, IDEA and/or similar software programs for data analysis

- Fidelis, ArcSight, Niksun, Websense, ProofPoint, BlueCoat and/or similar auditing and network defense tools

- Firewall and intrusion detection/prevention protocols

Soft Skills:

Brush up on your oral and written communication skills – a Security Auditor is often judged by the clarity and thoroughness of his/her reports. Employers will also be looking for candidates who aren't afraid of travel. Auditors frequently have to visit a wide variety of sites to gather data.

Certifications for Security Auditors

When it comes to auditing accreditations, the most valuable certification may be the CISA. We would also suggest looking into the CISSP. Both appear frequently in job requirements.

- **CISA:** Certified Information Systems Auditor

- **CISM:** Certified Information Security Manager

- **CISSP:** Certified Information Systems Security Professional

5.4. Types of Audits & approaches to Audits Technology based Audits:

What is an IT Audit?

An Information Technology (IT) audit is an audit of an organisation's IT systems, management, operations and related processes.

An IT audit may be carried out in connection with a financial statements (FS) audit, compliance or performance (Value-for-Money) audit. As the records, services and operations of many organisations are often highly computerised, there is a need to evaluate the IT controls in the course of an audit of these organisations.

Types of Audits:

The objectives of IT audits include:

- Evaluating the reliability of data from IT systems which have an impact on the financial statements of the organisations. (FS Audit)

- Ascertaining the level of compliance with the applicable laws, policies and standards in relation to IT. (Compliance Audit)

- Checking if there are instances of excess, extravagance, inefficiency and wastage in the use and management of IT systems. (Performance / Value-for-Money Audit)

Why is IT Audit important?

Many organisations are spending large amounts of money on IT because they recognise the tremendous benefits that IT can bring to their operations and services. However, they need to ensure that their IT systems are reliable, secure and not vulnerable to computer attacks.

IT audit is important because it gives assurance that the IT systems are adequately protected, provide reliable information to users and properly managed to achieve their intended benefits.

Many users rely on IT without knowing how the computers work. A computer error could be repeated indefinitely, causing more extensive damage than a human mistake.

IT audit could also help to reduce risks of data tampering, data loss or leakage, service disruption, and poor management of IT systems.

How is IT Audit carried out?

Generally, IT audit is carried out as follows:

1. Establish the IT audit objectives and scope.
2. Develop an audit plan to achieve the IT audit objectives.
3. Gather information on the relevant IT controls and evaluate them.
4. Perform audit tests, using Computer-Assisted Audit Techniques (CAATs) such as data extraction and analysis software or test data where appropriate.
5. Report on the IT audit findings.

In performing its IT audits, the Auditor-General's Office (AGO) also checks for compliance with the Government policies, standards, laws and regulations on information and related technology.

Where appropriate, AGO uses the IT audit tools, technical guides and other resources recommended by ISACA (Information Systems Audit & Control Association), and encourages staff to be certified as CISA (Certified Information Systems Auditor).

- **Types of Audit**

  - Audit can be an independent review. It can be financial statements, internal controls, any operation etc. Following are the types of review:

    a) Financial Audit or Conventional Audit

    b) Operational Audit

    c) Management Audit

    d) Environmental Audit

    e) Information System Audit

    f) Internal Audit

    g) External Audit

5.5. Vulnerability scanning and penetration testing:

Vulnerability Scanning:

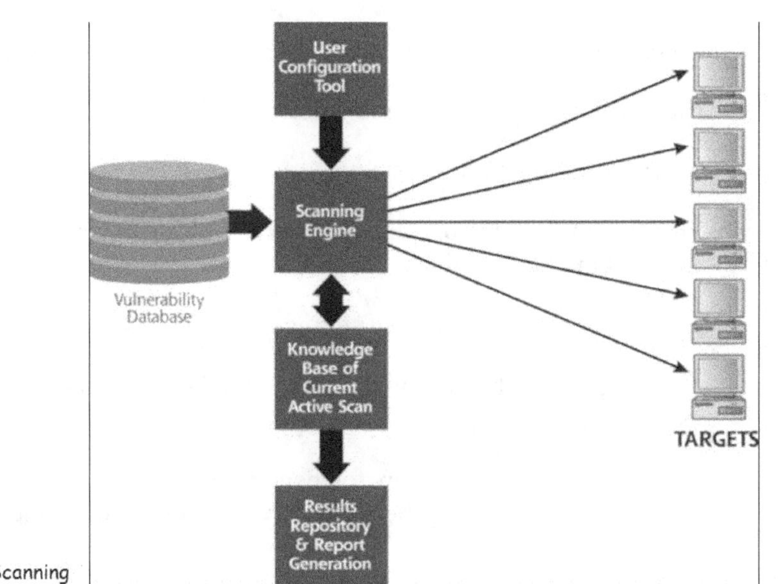

Vulnerability scanning identifies hosts and open ports, together with information on the associated vulnerabilities

  • Different to port scanning as doesn't rely on human interpretation of the results

  • Most vulnerability scanners also attempt to provide information on mitigating discovered vulnerabilities

  • Vulnerability scanners provide system and network administrators with proactive tools that can be used to identify vulnerabilities before an adversary can find them

  • A vulnerability scanner is a relatively fast and easy way to quantify an organization's exposure to surface vulnerabilities

211

• Vulnerability scanners can also help identify out-of-date software versions, applicable patches or system upgrades, and validate compliance with, or deviations from, the organization's security policy vulnerability scanners provide the following capabilities:

•Identifying active hosts on network

•Identifying active and vulnerable services (ports) on hosts.

•Identifying applications and banner grabbing.

•Identifying operating systems.

•Identifying vulnerabilities associated with discovered operating systems and applications.

•Identifying mis-configured settings.

•Testing compliance with host application usage/security policies.

•Establishing a foundation for penetration testing the following corrective actions may be necessary as a result of vulnerability scanning:

•Upgrade or patch vulnerable systems to mitigate identified vulnerabilities as appropriate

•Deploy mitigating measures if the system cannot be immediately patched in order to minimize the probability of this system being compromised

•Improve configuration management program and procedures to ensure that systems are upgraded routinely

•Assign a staff member to monitor vulnerability alerts and mailing lists, examine their applicability to the organization's environment and initiate appropriate system changes

•Modify the organization's security policies, architecture, or other documentation to ensure that security practices include timely system updates and upgrades.

Penetration Testing:

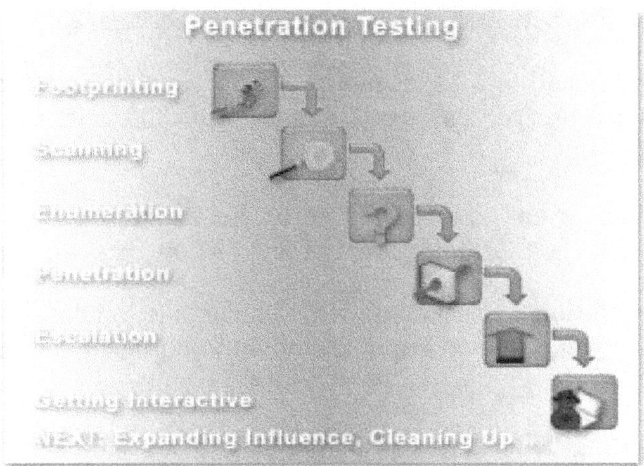

Penetration Testing is the "art" of legal or ethical hacking where a security specialist or team of specialists tests and documents the security or protection of a system by breaking into it, normally "no holds barred" with exception of very disruptive attacks that may effect critical business operations. These teams are often called a Red Team or a Tiger Team.

Get Permission:

Essential to Penetration Testing is to have a written permission that clearly defines that the person or team is allowed to perform the test and scope of the test. This is commonly refered to as a **Get out Of Jail Free Card** .The written permission should be signed by a high ranking officer. **E.g.** CISO, CIO or CEO, you should never start any **Penetration Testing.**

The 9 Steps:

The team will normally follow the exact same steps as the real attackers. These steps has been categorised into generic models of which the Foundstone authors of the Hacking Exposed book series has the most known and comprehensive. This model has the following components that are normally sequential but may be looping as well:

1. **Footprinting** - Determining the targets footprint, e.g. DNS records, IP scope, public information, contact information, etc.

2. **Scanning** - Determining the targets openings, e.g. service ports, wireless networks, modems pools, vpn servers, etc.

3. **Enumeration** - Determining the services behind the openings, e.g. webservers, systems, routers, firewalls, wifi authentication, etc.

4. **Penetration** - Selecting appropiate exploits and penetrate the target, e.g. SQL injection, buffer overflow, password attacks, etc.

5. **Escalation** - Escalation of the credentials to admin or root, e.g. dll injection, local exploit, configuration change, sceduled jobs, etc.

6. **Getting Interactive** - Getting a remote shell or GUI on the target, e.g. RDP, VNC, NetCat, etc.

7. **Expanding Influence** - Moving from the initial target as a foothold or beach-head to the rest of the network taking over the domain.

8. **Cleaning Up** - Ensuring backdoors and removing evidence, e.g. rootkits, log removal, log editing, etc.

9. **Reporting** - Writing and presenting a report on the pen-test to the owners of the network one had authorization to test.

Penetration testing is security testing in which evaluators attempt to circumvent the security features of a system based on their understanding of the system design and implementation.

    • The purpose of penetration testing is to identify methods of gaining access to a system by using common tools and techniques used by attackers

    • However, it is a very labor-intensive activity and requires great expertise to minimize the risk to targeted systems.

    • It may slow the organization's networks response time due to network scanning and vulnerability scanning.

These rules of engagement should include:

• Specific IP addresses/ranges to be tested

• Any restricted hosts (i.e., hosts, systems, subnets, not to be tested)

•A list of acceptable testing techniques (e.g. social engineering, DoS, etc.) and tools (password crackers, network sniffers, etc.)

• Times when testing is to be conducted (e.g., during business hours, after business hours, etc.)

• Identification of a finite period for testing

• IP addresses of the machines from which penetration testing will be conducted so that administrators can differentiate the legitimate penetration testing attacks from actual malicious attacks

• Points of contact for the penetration testing team, the targeted systems, and the networks

• Measures to prevent law enforcement being called with false alarms (created by the testing)

• Handling of information collected by penetration testing team

To simulate an actual external attack, the testers are not provided with any real information about the target environment other than targeted IPaddress/ranges and they must covertly collect information before the attack.

• An internal penetration test is similar to an external except that the testers are now on the internal network (i.e., behind the firewall) and are granted some level of access to the network (generally as a user but sometimes at a higher level).

• The penetration testers will then try to gain a greater level of access to the network through privilege escalation

5.6. Resistance to Audits:

Resistance to Security Audits have explained, so far, the benifits from security audits; however, some companies look at audits as the necessary evil. Planning for an audit requires accepting why auditing is good for the business and expecting to take the audits's finding as positive criticism and move forward. If security audits provide benefits to today's net-centric organization where digital assets are so valuable, one would think that getting regular security audits conducted is the default practice; the reality is far from this! Industry practice shows that most firms have regular financial audits. However, very few firms get regular, comprehensive technology security audits done. Give the critical importance of technology to today's organization, it is high time that organization reconsider their position on security audits. These are several reasons why firms do not prioritize security audits. Tipical ones to quote a few are given in Table no. 35.3 and counter arguments to overrule those objections are also provides. The message to readers is to have a positive and healthy attitude toward security audits.

To sum up, we say that organization should not fear security auditors; they should rather embrace there help and advice in order to make their organizations more secure to getting a handle of existing and potential weekness. Keeping business secure is the need of the hour given the increasing globalization of our business.

Why security audits are given lower priority	Counter-argument in favor of regular security audit practices
Too much dependence on technology: Firewalls are already in place and that is enough	Firewalls and other devices are simply tools to help provide security. They do not, by themselves, provide security. Using a castle as an analogy, think of firewalls and other such tools as simply the walls and watch towers. Without guards, reports and policies and procedures in place, they provide little protection
Perception problems: That security audits are not so important and the ignorance that, like financial auditors, security auditors may not be available in the marketplace. Management has a question 'Who can provide these services?'	Yes, you can hire security auditors. There are a number of reputed firms that can provide these services*
Low awareness about security audits: For example, typically the thoughts in the mind of management are – 'We do not know what a security audit entails. What should be covered in a security audit?'	Security audits, like financial audits, should be performed on a regular basis. Changes in staffing, technology, policies, etc., all demand rethinking and reshaping of the firm's security environment. Audits are an excellent forum for this
Often, management has thinking – 'We have already had a security audit. Why do we need another one?'	Security audits may be required as an ongoing activity.
The fear of the technical realm and management's insecurity –'We had a security audit but the report was too technical.'	A security audit report need not be overtly technical as to be incomprehensible to the firm's management committee. See section 'Context Section of the Penetration Testing Report'

*Note: In Section 35.14, we have provided some parameters to consider while selecting an external security auditor/security auditing

5.7. Key success factors for Security Audits:

Today's digital environment, cybersecurity is typically top of mind for company leaders. They often know enough to be concerned, but not enough to actually address those concerns. In other words, there is no question that cybersecurity is an area of high risk for most organizations, but how they should respond to this risk is unclear.

It is the job of the IT audit function to determine how the organization should respond to risks that are specific to their operation and then evaluate whether the response is appropriate based on auditing standards and best practices. One common response to mitigate risk is to implement countermeasures, also known as controls. In those situations it is the responsibility of the auditor to evaluate the effectiveness of the controls to determine if they will indeed work.

For example, business leaders often believe that a firewall is a sufficient response to cybersecurity concerns. Some questions IT auditors will ask these situations include, What type of firewall is it? How has it been configured? How often are the rules updated? The IT auditor will also inform senior management that a firewall is only one of many controls that should be considered when responding to the threat of a cyberattack.

While the audit team should be actively involved in the tactical procedures of auditing the company, a skilled audit team that partners with the board of directors and senior management will not only identify aspects of the company that need attention, but also develop an audit plan that supports the organization's overall strategy and act as consultants to help move the company closer to its vision. Over time, with the ongoing involvement of the audit team on the tactical and strategic levels, the organization can certainly count audit as one of its key success factors.

ormation Security Audit services to medium and large organizations with a particular focus on Compliance Audits as well as Business Process Audits.

The service is aimed at identifying potential security threats and vulnerabilities that may be compromised and eventually could impact the confidentiality, integrity or availability of your organization's information assets. Versos technical security audit methodology has been developed in accordance with International Information Systems Audit Standards (ISACA).

With a proven track record conducting Information Security Audits at numerous prestigious organizations in the Middle East, we are confident that our Audit services will provide your organization with and effective and valuable service that will meet your expectations.

Information Security Audit Objectives

•	To systematically and proactively protect your organization from the dangers and potential costs of computer misuse, data leakage and cybercrime.

• To control and manage costs related to information security.

• To provide credibility within your organization as well as with your customers and partners.

• To provide better compliance with regulatory requirements for security and privacy.

• To provide your organization with informed and practical decisions about security technologies and solutions applicable to your environment.

Our Information Security Audit approach

Versos Information Security Auditors and Consultants work with you as partner sharing the same objective and that is to ensure that your information is indeed secure.

Versos methodology comprises five major steps. The steps are engineered in a comprehensive, shortest path and systematic approach. The major steps are:

•	**Planning**

> Definition of the scope
>
> Assigning the key resources
>
> Developing the audit plan

- **Audit**

  Conducting walkthroughs and interviews

  Reviewing and examining existing policies and procedures

  Conduct the necessary tests

  Identify the potential issues

- **Vulnerability Assessment**

  Data Collection and Identification

  Network Mapping and Enumeration

  Vulnerability Scanning

  Risk Level and Impact Analysis

- **Reporting**

  Audit result analysis

  Audit result report

  Mitigation report

  Audit presentation

- **Mitigation**

  Work with your organization to help mitigate the risks

  Offer proven solutions that mitigate the risks

Our Success factors

To ensure a successful audit, we:

- Provide industry specific expert consultants

- Understand the need for bilingual consultants (Arabic & English) to conduct audits

- Have open communications and a shared focus with you

- Proactively suggest as well as offer to implement the mitigation

  Recommendations resulting from the audit